TIRPITZ IN NORWAY

X-craft midget submarines raid the fjords, Operation *Source* 1943

ANGUS KONSTAM

OSPREY PUBLISHING
Bloomsbury Publishing Plc
PO Box 883, Oxford, OX1 9PL, UK
1385 Broadway, 5th Floor, New York, NY 10018, USA
E-mail: info@ospreypublishing.com
www.ospreypublishing.com

OSPREY is a trademark of Osprey Publishing Ltd

First published in Great Britain in 2019

A catalogue record for this book is available from the British Library.

ISBN: PB 9781472835857; eBook 9781472835864;
ePDF 9781472835840; XML 9781472835871

19 20 21 22 23 10 9 8 7 6 5 4 3 2 1

Battlescenes by Edouard A Groult
Cover art by Adam Tooby
Maps by www.bounford.com
3D BEV by Alan Gilliland
Index by Zoe Ross
Typeset by PDQ Digital Media Solutions, Bungay, UK
Printed and bound in India by Replika Press Private Ltd.

Osprey Publishing supports the Woodland Trust, the UK's leading woodland conservation charity.

To find out more about our authors and books visit www.ospreypublishing.com. Here you will find extracts, author interviews, details of forthcoming events and the option to sign up for our newsletter.

PHOTOGRAPHS

All the photographs in this book are courtesy of the Stratford Archive.

COVER ART

On the morning of 22 September 1943 the battleship *Tirpitz*, the most powerful warship in the German fleet, was lying peaceably at anchor in the Kaafjord, near the northernmost tip of Norway. Then, at 8.12am, two huge explosions erupted beneath the keel of the German battleship. She was lifted bodily into the air, and for a few seconds the ship quivered from stem to stern. The *Tirpitz* then began listing to port as water flooded into her hull. Two of her gun turrets were put out of action, and her propulsion system was irreparably damaged. The pride of the German Kriegsmarine had been put out of action. The damage was caused by four explosive charges laid by two British midget submarines – X-Craft – in what was widely regarded as one of the most daring submarine operations of the entire war. (Cover art by Adam Tooby)

CONTENTS

INTRODUCTION

In September 1943, the British Home Fleet's most pressing task was the protection of the Arctic Convoys. Earlier in the war, this maritime lifeline between Britain and Russia's northern ports played a vital role in containing the German invasion of the Soviet Union. American and British aircraft, guns, tanks and trucks shipped to Murmansk or Archangel helped stem the German tide. Now, in mid-1943, the Soviets were on the offensive, and while the convoys were less important militarily, their strategic import was immense as a tangible display of Allied cooperation. So the Home Fleet continued to protect these vital convoys, particularly as they passed within reach of German-occupied Norway.

During 1940 the Germans had developed air and naval bases in Norway, so when the Arctic Convoys began the following summer, the German navy, or Kriegsmarine, was well-placed to attack them. The number of air and U-boat attacks increased steadily during 1941–42. Then, to step up the pressure, the battleship *Tirpitz*, the sister-ship of the ill-fated *Bismarck*, was ordered to Norway. While she only made the occasional sortie, the very presence of *Tirpitz* posed a serious latent threat to the Allied war effort. Urged by Prime Minister Winston Churchill, the British made several attempts to neutralise *Tirpitz*, first through air attacks and then by 'human torpedoes'. These were all unsuccessful, and in early 1943, when *Tirpitz* moved further north to the Altenfjord, her new base lay beyond the reach of British-based heavy bombers. Another way had to be found to put the mighty battleship out of action.

Fortunately for the Royal Navy, it now had the craft and the men needed for just this kind of operation. A small batch of midget submarines, known as X-craft, had been developed for just this sort of mission, and their crews had been training hard. The decision was made to launch Operation *Source* – an underwater attack on the *Tirpitz* using the X-craft. In September 1943, six X-craft were towed across the Norwegian Sea by submarines, with four of them released off the entrance to the Altenfjord. The X-craft then crept

up the heavily guarded fjord towards the battleship's lair. However, only two of the midget submarines were able to breach the *Tirpitz*'s underwater defences. They were then able to lay their underwater explosive charges before being forced to the surface and their crews captured. However, their charges detonated soon afterwards, and the resulting blast put the *Tirpitz* out of action for several critical months. It also ended the latent threat the battleship posed to the Arctic Convoys. Despite being costly in both boats lost and crew killed or captured, the raid was therefore deemed to be a major success. It was also one of the greatest submarine attacks of the war – even the German admiral in charge of the stricken battleship praised the courage and enterprise of the British submariners. This is the story of that daring operation, and of the men who risked all to sink the *Tirpitz*.

The midget submarine *X-10* under tow by the submarine *Sceptre*, with her passage crew commander Sub-Lieutenant Page standing on the coaming. The photograph was taken during towing trials in Loch Cairnbawn, during the final days before Operation *Source* began.

INITIAL STRATEGY

At 3.15am on 22 June 1941, Nazi Germany and its allies launched Operation *Barbarossa* – the invasion of the Soviet Union. The Soviets were singularly unprepared for the assault, and for the scale of the air attacks which accompanied it. The Red Air Force was all but destroyed, and with complete air superiority the German tanks rolled eastwards, breaking through all lines of resistance and surrounding huge pockets of Russian troops as they went. The infantry following them mopped up these pockets and dealt with any Soviet attempts to counter-attack, or to escape destruction. In just over two months the invaders had swept through the Baltic States, Byelorussia and large parts of the Ukraine. Novgorod and Smolensk had been captured, and the Germans were poised to do the same to both Leningrad and Kiev. However, the advance was slowing. Despite spectacular German advances and the staggering Russian losses, Soviet resistance was stiffening, while the Germans were running short of supplies.

The Arctic Convoys

By August the Soviets were also running short of the military tools they needed. The situation was fast becoming critical, as the Russians found themselves unable to replace the thousands of tanks, guns and aircraft they had lost. By then many Soviet production centres were overrun, while many others were being transported eastwards beyond the Urals, out of the path of the German advance. It would take time for these to start producing war materiel again. In the meantime, Soviet soldiers and airmen were having to stem the German tide with the limited weaponry they had left. It was at this point that Stalin demanded that the Western Allies do what they could to help. Prime Minister Churchill agreed to provide essential war materiel – tanks, aircraft, guns and trucks – although ammunition and fuel were also provided. Tanks and aircraft were especially welcomed.

The British were desperately short of war materiel themselves. While the imminent threat of a cross-Channel invasion had receded, British troops

The midget submarine *X-5* being prepared for the operation on board HMS *Bonaventure*. This was done on 5 September, while the support vessel was anchored in Loch Cairnbawn. The X-craft's port side charge can be clearly seen, containing 2 tons of Amatex explosive. *X-5* was sunk with all hands in the Kaafjord during the attack.

were heavily involved in the war being waged in North Africa, and in the Central and Eastern Mediterranean. Still, Churchill realized the vital strategic importance of supporting the Soviet Union. If Russia could be kept in the war, then Germany would be increasingly drawn into a fight which ultimately it would be unable to win. In mid-1941, Britain was unable to spare the troops needed to provide direct military support. However, Churchill was determined to provide whatever help he could in the form of war materiel. While these could be shipped through Persia, this roundabout supply route would take time to establish. A more direct link was needed, one that took advantage of Britain's main strategic asset – its control of the sea.

The decision was made to establish a maritime supply line between Britain and the Soviet Union. This meant the ports of northern Russia – Archangel and Murmansk – the first of which was icebound for part of the year. The original intention was that Soviet-registered merchant ships would carry the goods, but there simply weren't enough of them to do the job. British merchant ships were used instead, augmented by a handful of ships operating under the flag of other European countries. The result in August 1941 was the establishment of the Arctic Convoys – a strategic lifeline that demonstrated a joint Allied commitment to prevail in the struggle to the death with Nazi Germany. Four months later, when the United States entered the war, they wholeheartedly

The submarine depot ship HMS *Titania* (Commander William Fell), anchored in Loch Cairnbawn before the commencement of Operation *Source*. She first saw service during World War I, and between the wars she was stationed in Hong Kong. She joined the midget submarine flotilla to provide support for the towing submarines.

The principal target of Operation *Source* – the German battleship *Tirpitz*, seen here shortly before Operation *Source* as she lay behind her anti-torpedo net enclosure in the Kaafjord. It can be seen, forming a box-like enclosure, secured to the shore in two places. A gate off the battleship's port bow provided easy access in and out of the enclosure for small boats.

supported the enterprise. Eventually, American ships would outnumber British ones in the convoys, while American war materiel made up the bulk of the cargo carried by the convoys.

The first Arctic Convoy sailed from Iceland on 21 August 1941. Codenamed Operation *Dervish*, this was a limited undertaking, the convoy consisting of just five merchant ships and a tanker. The escort consisted of destroyers, minesweepers and armed trawlers, with distant support provided by a task force from the Home Fleet. The merchant ships carried rubber, tin, fuel and 15 Hawker Hurricane fighters, accompanied by a Royal Air Force detachment to operate the aircraft and to train the Russians in their use. This first Arctic Convoy arrived in Archangel on 31 August without suffering any losses. It would be the first of many such convoys, either outward bound from Iceland and later from northern Scotland, or homeward bound, sailing from either Archangel or Murmansk. Eventually 78 convoys would make this hazardous voyage, running the gauntlet of attacks from German aircraft and warships based in occupied Norway.

It was certainly a hazardous voyage – Churchill dubbed it 'the worst journey in the world'. First of all, these convoys were seasonal, as the long summer hours of daylight made them too vulnerable to attack from German aircraft. The convoys would keep as far from Norway as they could, but far beyond the Arctic Circle they encountered the edge of the pack ice, which crept southwards with the onset of winter. It also meant that as they entered the Barents Sea beyond Norway, they had no option but to come within range of German airfields. Essentially, the pack ice and the Norwegian coast acted as a funnel which constricted the convoys. This was where the air attacks took place, or where the U-boats lay in wait. These dangers increased when the Germans deployed a powerful group of surface warships in northern Norway – ships that included the *Tirpitz*. The convoys remained in extreme danger until they reached the Kola Inlet, marking the seaward approaches to Murmansk.

Then there was the weather. Setting aside the risk of being bombed or torpedoed, these Allied sailors faced an equally dangerous threat from nature itself. First there was the bitter cold, where the build-up of ice threatened to make ships capsize or stopped guns from working. Conditions on the upper deck could be brutal, but it was often little better below decks, where both water and plumbing pipes froze, and the ships' heating rarely kept the men warm. The seas themselves were treacherous, with gales all too frequent, while the near-perpetual darkness of the winter months was disorientating. If anyone ended up in the icy sea, their chances of survival were minimal, while even those who made it into a lifeboat faced a lingering death from hypothermia unless they were rescued quickly. Still, the fate of the Allied cause was at stake, so most sailors faced these dangers with a stoic determination. They saw it as their job, and they knew the high stakes.

The German response

The Germans were slow to react to the creation of these convoys. The first seven outward-bound convoys made it to Archangel or Murmansk without incident. So too did the first few homeward-bound ones. The Kriegsmarine had already stationed U-boats in northern Norway, but at first these were focused on the campaign in the Atlantic. It took time to reposition the boats into the likely path of these new convoys. It had been almost a year since the Germans completed the conquest of Norway, but they had been slow to develop it as a forward base for both the Kriegsmarine and the Luftwaffe (German Air Force). Strategically, they needed control of Norway's inland waterways to ensure the flow of Swedish iron ore from Narvik to ports in Germany. That, though, could be protected by a few aircraft and light naval forces.

The capture of Norway also forced the British to abandon their blockade line between Norway and Scotland. That placed a significant burden on the Home Fleet, re-establishing a much longer patrol line beyond the reach of the Luftwaffe. That meant patrols between Greenland and Iceland, as well as from Iceland to the Faroes, and from there to the mainland of Britain by way of Orkney and Shetland. It also made it easier for German

An X-craft surfacing in Scottish waters after a training dive. Visible in this photo is the small night periscope, protected by a periscope guard which also served as an extra handrail. Astern of it is the base of the attack periscope, which is fully retracted in this photograph. In Operation *Source* the mooring eye at the bow was used to secure the towing rope during the passage to Norway.

U-boats and surface warships to slip through these patrol lines, and so enter the North Atlantic. However, it was the commencement of the Arctic Convoys that really opened German eyes to the full strategic importance of Norway. The only way either the Kriegsmarine or Luftwaffe could disrupt this new sea route was to attack it using aircraft, U-boats and surface warships based in Norway. That was the reason why, in January 1942, Germany's largest battleship arrived in Norwegian waters.

The *Tirpitz*

The arrival of the German battleship *Tirpitz* off the Trondheimsfjord in mid-January 1942 marked a new strategic direction for the Kriegsmarine. She had been sent there to form the core of a powerful naval surface group, whose task was to disrupt the Arctic Convoys. Her first Norwegian base was in the Faettenfjord, some 75 miles from the open sea and 16 miles north-east of Trondheim. This was still around 700 miles from the convoy route, but it was close enough to pose a major threat. Later, in March 1943, the battleship would move further north, to the Kaafjord, a spur of the larger Altenfjord near North Cape, the most northerly tip of Norway. It was also 75 miles from the sea. This, of course, provided security, as the approaches to the battleship's lair could be protected by booms, nets and patrol boats, as well as by flak guns, shore-based radar stations and smoke generators. In both anchorages, the steep-sided narrow fjord the battleship used as an anchorage also made it extremely difficult to attack from the air. The result was the creation of two forward naval bases which both sides saw as all but impregnable to attack from the sea or air.

The *Tirpitz*, however, wasn't the only major German warship to be sent to Norway. The battleship *Scharnhorst* was also there, and while she lacked the *Tirpitz*'s firepower and armour, she was still a fairly formidable capital ship. So too were the armoured cruisers *Lützow* (formerly the *Deutschland*) and the *Admiral Scheer*, which were what the British called 'pocket battleships', with the armour of a heavy cruiser but the guns of a capital ship. Then there were the heavy cruisers *Prinz Eugen* and *Admiral Hipper*, as well a supporting flotilla of destroyers and other smaller craft such as minesweepers and patrol vessels. It all amounted to a powerful naval force, and one based within easy striking range of the Arctic Convoys. The *Tirpitz*, though, was the deadliest of all of these. Like her sister ship the *Bismarck*, the *Tirpitz* was a modern

The *Tirpitz*, pictured while lying in the Faettenfjord, an eastern arm of the Trondheimsfjord. She was moved from this secure base to the Kaafjord in March 1943, so she could be closer to the route taken by the Arctic Convoys.

battleship, with the potential to outfight any battleship the Royal Navy could send against her. As a result, the *Tirpitz* became something of a 'bogeyman' for the British, who were forced to keep sufficient naval power in northern waters in order to neutralize the threat she posed.

This was the real essence of the battleship's role. In the late 19th century the American naval strategist Alfred Thayer Mahan (1840–1914) became highly influential, the impact of his theories on naval warfare helping to dictate strategy. One of those theories was his notion of how a naval force could influence the course of a war without even leaving port. He called it 'a fleet in being', as its mere presence forced the enemy to tie down resources to counter it. If it sortied from port and was beaten, then its influence would be lost. However, by remaining 'in being', then it continued to dictate naval operations in that theatre. A prime example of this was the German High Seas Fleet during World War I. While it lacked the numbers of Britain's Grand Fleet, it forced the British to keep their own fleet in readiness, to counter any sortie the Germans made. So, just like the High Seas Fleet had done a quarter of a century before, *Tirpitz* and the other German warships in Norway formed a powerful Mahanian 'fleet in being', tying down the British Home Fleet in the same way that the Grand Fleet had been during the previous war.

As for the *Tirpitz* herself, while her career was overshadowed by her ill-fated sister ship *Bismarck*, in the early summer of 1941 she became the most powerful warship in European waters. The idea behind the Bismarck class of battleships was that until the mid-1930s, the German Reichsmarine (State Navy) was constrained by the terms of the Treaty of Versailles (1919). Until the treaty was abrogated by the Reichsführer Adolf Hitler in March 1935, Germany was forbidden to build battleships. The Anglo-German Naval Agreement signed that same year effectively issued a stamp of approval on German naval expansion – something that was

The launching of the battleship *Tirpitz* in Wilhelmshaven on 1 April 1939. The ceremony was attended by Führer and Reichskanzler Adolf Hitler, but the launch itself was performed by a daughter of Grand Admiral Tirpitz, founder of the old Imperial German Navy.

already well underway. Before pulling out of the treaty, Germany had built three *panzerschiffe* (armoured ships). While the British dubbed the *Deutschland*, *Graf Spee* and *Admiral Scheer* 'pocket battleships', they were really powerful cruisers, but ones which carried six 28cm (11in) guns apiece.

These were followed by two larger capital ships, whose plans were drawn up in secret as they broke the terms of the Treaty of Versailles. These two ships would become the battlecruisers *Scharnhorst* and *Gneisenau*, displacing over 35,000 tons apiece and armed with nine 28cm guns. While they lacked the armour of a modern battleship, and the British thus classified them as 'battlecruisers', they were really battleships, as they were as well protected as many older British capital ships. What followed was even more ambitious. During the last years of World War I, a pair of Bayern-class 'super-dreadnoughts' entered service. These carried 38cm (15in) guns, and were designed to counter the latest British 'fast battleships', which mounted the same calibre of gun. Although in the 1930s the Bayern class no longer existed, their plans did, as did the technical designs for their ordnance. These could therefore be used as blueprints for a new and even more powerful warship.

In 1935, when the Reichsmarine changed its name to the Kriegsmarine (battle fleet), a major naval expansion programme was begun. This involved the building of a range of warships, from capital ships to minesweepers, patrol craft and U-boats. At the same time, these old battleship plans were dusted off and work began on designing a new class of battleship. Officially, this scheme was known as the *Schiffbauersatzplan* (Replacement Ship Construction Programme). The idea was that the ageing pre-dreadnought battleships in the German fleet would be replaced by more modern capital ships. The first of these battleship building projects was dubbed *Schlachtschiff* 'F' *Ersatz Hannover* (Battleship 'F', *Hannover* Replacement). Yet this would be no mere replacement. Instead, what Dr Hermann Burkhardt (1881–1969), Chief of the Department of Ship Construction, produced was the most powerful battleship afloat.

Work on Battleship 'F' began in July 1936: she would eventually become the *Bismarck*. Then, on 20 October, the keel of Battleship 'G' was laid down in the naval shipyard in Wilhelmshaven: she would eventually become the *Tirpitz*. The design of these Bismarck-class battleships had been a difficult process, as the Kriegsmarine kept changing the design, tinkering with different calibres of guns, more armour and a different propulsion system. In the end, though, the design was constrained by the need to transit the Kaiser Wilhelm Canal, which limited their beam and draught, and by the availability

After the loss of her sister ship *Bismarck* in May 1941, *Tirpitz* became the most powerful warship in the Kriegsmarine. Here she is shown during the summer of 1941, while 'working up' – conducting crew training exercises in the Baltic.

of suitable ordnance. *Bismarck* was launched in Hamburg on St Valentine's Day 1939, and *Tirpitz* entered the water six weeks later, on 1 April. Hitler watched her launch, as did a huge crowd of Nazi leaders, dignitaries and shipyard workers. Fitting her out took almost two years, but *Tirpitz* was finally commissioned into the Kriegsmarine on 25 February 1941.

For a few brief weeks, *Bismarck* and *Tirpitz* were both in Gotenhafen (Gdynia in Poland), where they were 'working up' – preparing the ships and crews for full operational duties. Then, in late May the *Bismarck* began her sortie into the Atlantic, accompanied by the heavy cruiser *Prinz Eugen*. On the morning of 24 May, *Bismarck*'s guns sank the British battlecruiser *Hood* in the Battle of the Denmark Strait, fought between Iceland and Greenland. Then, on the evening of 26 May *Bismarck* was attacked by Swordfish torpedo bombers flying from the fleet carrier *Ark Royal*, one of the torpedoes damaging her steering mechanism and rudder. As a result the *Bismarck* was crippled, and two battleships of the Home Fleet were able to intercept her. Early on 27 May, *Bismarck* was sunk in action, and all but a handful of her crew were lost. That day, *Tirpitz* became the largest capital ship in the German navy.

Captain Karl Topp and his crew planned to complete their training before the end of June, in time to support the German invasion of the Soviet Union. However, problems with the battleship's fire-control systems led to a delay. It was late September before *Tirpitz* became fully operational. She then joined the Baltic Fleet, which bottled up its Soviet counterpart in its base at Kronstadt. The original plan was for *Tirpitz* to conduct its own sortie into the Atlantic, but the loss of *Bismarck* forced the German Naval Command to reconsider this scheme. Grandadmiral Erich Raeder, commander-in-chief of the Kriegsmarine, decided to use her as the centrepiece of a 'fleet in being', based in Norwegian waters. That way she could tie down powerful units of the Home Fleet, without the undue risk involved in an operation in the North Atlantic. The future of *Tirpitz* was decided – she would be sent to Norway.

Tirpitz certainly was a powerful addition to the Kriegsmarine naval group being assembled there. She displaced 42,900 tons – slightly more than *Bismarck* – and was a large battleship – over 820ft long, with a beam of 118ft – so could just squeeze through the Kaiser Wilhelm Canal, but with mere inches to spare. As for armament, her appearance was fairly conventional. Like the earlier Bayern-class 'super-dreadnoughts', she mounted eight 38cm (15in) guns in four twin turrets. Following German convention, the two forward ones were named 'Anton' and 'Bruno', while the pair aft became 'Caesar' and 'Dora'. The guns were a new design, rather than a direct copy of their World War I forebears, and more importantly were aimed using the latest in optical rangefinders, supported by analogue computers which were used to provide firing solutions. These were modern guns, with the potential to fire a shell weighing four-fifths of a ton up to 20 nautical miles.

Her secondary armament of 12 15cm (6in) guns were mounted in six twin turrets, three on each beam. *Tirpitz* also carried a formidable array of flak guns: 16 10.5cm (4.1in) ones in eight twin mounts, 16 3.7cm (1.5in) medium flak guns, also in twin mountings, and an array of 20mm (0.8in) light anti-aircraft guns. Strangely, she also carried a pair of quadruple torpedo launchers. In Norway, this formidable array of anti-aircraft protection was augmented by a host of flak guns placed around the battleship's lairs. As for protection, *Tirpitz* had an armoured belt 32cm (12.5in) thick, which tapered below the waterline and towards the bow and stern. The belt also formed an armoured citadel, protecting the battleship's vitals – her machinery spaces and her magazines. She had torpedo bulkheads – an inner layer of armour designed to protect the ship from direct torpedo hits. However, if *Tirpitz* had an Achilles Heel, it lay below the waterline, where underwater protection was relatively light.

Tirpitz was a formidable fighting machine, and her presence in Norway forced Admiral Tovey, commanding the British Home Fleet, to keep a force of two or three battleships at sea to cover the Arctic Convoy sailings. These usually included his own flagship *King George V*. It also meant keeping one or two fleet carriers in readiness, even though all these ships were desperately needed elsewhere – particularly in the Mediterranean and Pacific theatres. The need for this British naval force was demonstrated in March 1942, when *Tirpitz* and three destroyers made a sortie from the Faettenfjord in an attempt to intercept convoy PQ-12.

This sortie, codenamed Operation *Sportpalast*, wasn't a success, as Admiral Ciliax in *Tirpitz* couldn't locate the Allied convoy. Admiral Tovey tried to intercept him, but Ciliax, Germany's battleships commander, broke off the operation before battle was joined. All the British managed was a half-hearted air attack on *Tirpitz*, carried out by Swordfish torpedo bombers flying from the carrier *Victorious*.

Tirpitz was clearly a significant threat to the convoys, so in late March RAF heavy bombers conducted the first of three bombing attacks on *Tirpitz* as she lay in the Faettenfjord. The liberal use of smoke screened the battleship, so only one of the 34 Halifax bombers found the target, and its bombs missed their target. Five aircraft were lost in the mission.

Undeterred, the RAF tried again on two consecutive evenings in late April. Once again the bombers had problems locating their target, and all of their bombs missed. The RAF lost another seven bombers in the missions. RAF Bomber Command gave up the attempt, declaring that a combination of the local terrain and the battleship's defences rendered *Tirpitz* immune to successful attack from the air. The British had to come up with another way of striking at *Tirpitz*. Meanwhile, the German battleship continued to menace the convoys.

KMS Tirpitz | Bismarck-class battleship	
Built	Kriegsmarinewerft, Wilhelmshaven
Laid Down	2 November 1936
Launched	1 April 1939
Commissioned	25 February 1941
Length	823ft 6in (251m) overall
Beam	118ft 1in (36m)
Draught	30ft 6in (9.3m) standard lading
Displacement	45,474 tonnes (50,425 tonnes fully laden)
Propulsion	Three Brown-Boveri geared turbines, 12 Wagner high-pressure boilers, powering three propellers and generating 160,796 steam horse power (shp)
Maximum Speed	30 knots
Range	8,870 nautical miles at 19 knots.
Armament (1942)	Eight 38cm (15in) SK/C-34 main guns in four twin turrets
	Twelve 15cm (6in) SK/L-55 secondary guns in six twin turrets
	Sixteen 10.5cm (4.1in) SK/C-33 heavy flak guns in eight twin mounts
	Sixteen 3.7cm (1.5in) SK/C-30 medium flak guns in eight twin mounts
	Twelve 2cm (0.8in) Flak 30 light flak guns in 12 single mounts
	Eight 53.3cm (21in) torpedoes in two quadruple mounts
Aircraft	Four Arado 196 A-3 reconnaissance float planes, one catapult
Sensors	FuMo23 'radar', Gruppenhorchgerät (GHG) hydrophone system
Protection	Belt: 320mm (13in)
	Turrets: 360mm (14in)
	Armoured Deck: 100–120mm (3.9–4.7in)
	Upper Deck: 50mm (2in)
Complement	2,608 officers and men (1943)

On 21 June 1942 convoy PQ-17 left Hvalfjord in Iceland, bound for Archangel. The 35 merchant ships were protected by the convoy's own escorts, as well as a 'distant covering force' of two battleships – one British and one American – accompanied by the carrier *Victorious* and several cruisers and destroyers. The convoy was sighted by a U-boat on 30 June, then shadowed by German reconnaissance planes. This presented new German fleet commander Admiral Schniewind with an opportunity to strike. He initiated Operation *Rösselsprung* (named after the knight's move in chess), an attack on the convoy spearheaded by *Tirpitz* and the armoured cruiser *Lützow*. The surface units failed to make contact as the force was recalled to its assembly point in the Altenfjord before it reached the convoy. However, the sortie proved enough of a threat for the Admiralty to order PQ-17 to scatter.

In May 1942 the Kriegsmarine's naval battle group in Norwegian waters sortied to attack an Arctic Convoy, PQ-17. *Tirpitz* took part in the operation, but the battle group was recalled before it could make contact with the Allied convoy or its escorts. This photograph, taken from a German destroyer, shows two members of the battle group, the armoured cruisers *Lützow* followed by her sister *Admiral Scheer*.

What followed was the single largest disaster to befall an Allied convoy during the war. A total of 24 merchant ships were lost to U-boat and air attacks during the days that followed. Only 11 made it safely into a Russian port. Winston Churchill described the destruction of PQ-17 as 'one of the most melancholy naval episodes of the entire war'. It came about because the Allies were unprepared for the German sortie and Admiral Tovey's covering force was too far away from PQ-17 to intervene. The decision to scatter, made by the British First Sea Lord Sir Dudley Pound, was still one of the most controversial commands issued during the naval war. Afterwards the *Tirpitz*, dubbed by her crew the 'Lonely Queen of the North', returned to her lair in the Faettenfjord.

If anything, the sortie magnified the threat she posed. It is little wonder that shortly afterwards, Churchill declared: 'The greatest single act to restore the balance of naval power would be the destruction or even the crippling of the *Tirpitz*.' He added: 'No other target is comparable to it.' The trouble was, if the RAF dubbed *Tirpitz* all but invulnerable to air attacks, the Royal Navy were equally hamstrung, as the ship's lair was far from the sea, up a fjord protected by coastal batteries. That effectively ruled out a surface attack. Even an attempt by conventional submarines was considered prohibitively dangerous due to the anti-submarine defences which lay between the Faettenfjord and the sea. With all conventional avenues closed to them, and encouraged by Churchill, the Admiralty began considering more unusual means of dealing with *Tirpitz*. Fortunately for them, they already had the men and the machines they needed to undertake such a hazardous enterprise.

THE PLAN

Chariots and Midgets

In October 1901 the Royal Navy's first submarine was launched. Christened *Holland I* after her designer John Holland, she bore more of a resemblance to the X-craft of 1943 than the more conventional submarines which followed her. Displacing just over 100 tons, manned by eight men and with an overall length of just under 64ft, *Holland I* could dive to 100ft and was powered by both electric and petrol engines. She was fitted with a torpedo tube, and so in theory she had an offensive capability, although she never launched a torpedo in anger. Instead she foundered in 1913, while on the way to the breaker's yard. *Holland I* was soon followed by larger submarines, and by the start of World War I the Royal Navy's submarine service comprised over 60 boats.

During the war, designs for a midget submarine were developed, but these plans never came to fruition. Between the wars, the Admiralty saw no need for craft of this type. It was only in the late 1930s that it reconsidered its stance, permitting the development of small underwater craft capable of sinking enemy warships in waters where larger submarines would be unable to enter. Meanwhile, the Italian Navy was developing small submersibles of their own. These craft were dubbed 'human torpedoes', as essentially that's what they were – a torpedo fitted with enlarged propellers, and ridden by two divers. Its compressed air propulsion system gave it a range of up to 10 nautical miles, and upon reaching its target the divers could attack it using magnetic explosive charges, which they clamped to the underside of the target's hull. They would then make their escape before detonating the charges.

The effectiveness of this Italian vessel was demonstrated on 19 December 1941, when Italian 'human torpedoes' penetrated the underwater defences of the naval base of Alexandria in Egypt – home of the British Mediterranean Fleet. The operation was a great success. When they detonated, the explosive

The prototype midget submarine *X-3*, pictured during trials in the Solent in the summer of 1942. Conning her from the after hatch is Major Millis Jefferis, a Royal Engineer seconded to the Admiralty to help develop the X-craft programme.

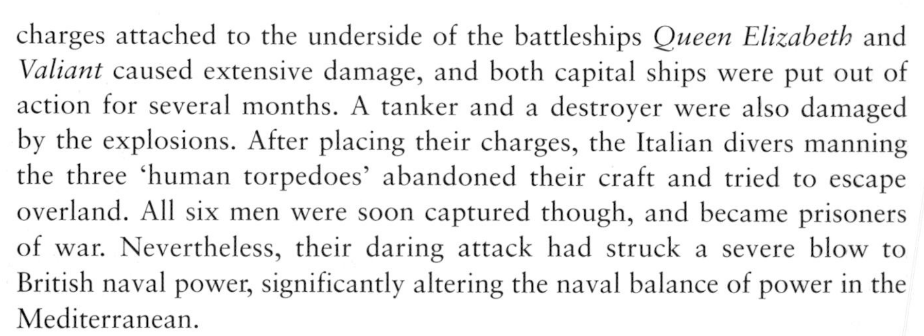

charges attached to the underside of the battleships *Queen Elizabeth* and *Valiant* caused extensive damage, and both capital ships were put out of action for several months. A tanker and a destroyer were also damaged by the explosions. After placing their charges, the Italian divers manning the three 'human torpedoes' abandoned their craft and tried to escape overland. All six men were soon captured though, and became prisoners of war. Nevertheless, their daring attack had struck a severe blow to British naval power, significantly altering the naval balance of power in the Mediterranean.

A 'human torpedo', or Chariot Mark I, being hoisted out of the water. Although she lacks her warhead, which was detachable and fitted to her bow, and also the after tail with its rudder and propeller, the positions for the two crew are clearly visible.

Less than a month later, on 18 January, Churchill demanded of his military Chiefs of Staff: 'Please report what is being done to emulate the exploits of the Italians in Alexandria Harbour, and similar methods of this kind. At the beginning of the war Colonel Jefferis had a number of bright ideas on the subject, which received little encouragement. Is there any reason why we should be incapable of the same kind of scientific aggressive action that the Italians have shown?' Millis Jefferis was actually a major at the time, a Royal Engineer, who had been seconded to the Navy in July 1940 to help develop plans for small submersibles. In this he was assisted by Commander Cromwell Varley, an experienced submariner. Together the two men would begin designing the midget submarines (or 'X-craft') which, in September 1943, would carry out the attack on the *Tirpitz*.

Meanwhile, the Navy were developing human torpedoes of their own. The Chiefs of the General Staff passed Churchill's demand to the Admiralty, who duly ordered Vice-Admiral Max Horton to come up with something. Horton was the commander of the Navy's submarine fleet. He in turn summoned Commander

William Fell, an experienced submariner, and ordered him to: 'Go away and build me a human torpedo ... and report to me as soon as you've got something.' Fell, nicknamed 'Tiny' due to his large frame, established himself in HMS *Dolphin*, the submarine shore base in Gosport, Hampshire. There he was joined by Commander Geoffrey Sladen, another veteran submariner, who had recently developed a diving suit and breathing apparatus. His diving apparatus was a 'closed-system' where the pure oxygen it supplied was recycled, rather than being exhaled. That way it didn't release a stream of bubbles to betray the diver's position.

Divers being helped out of a half-submerged Chariot Mark I after a practice dive. Their tight-fitting but cumbersome rubber diving suits and their oxygen breathing apparatus made it difficult to move without assistance when they emerged from the water.

While Sladen recruited volunteers, and trained them to use his diving equipment, Fell built a prototype 'human torpedo' using a large timber log strapped with diving weights. The volunteer divers were soon being towed underwater on this contraption, while Fell set about designing the real thing. Fortunately, he already had the plans of a captured Italian one. By June 1942 a working prototype was ready, but rather than calling it a 'human torpedo', Fell labelled it a 'Chariot'. Superficially, the Chariot Mark I resembled a British 21in torpedo. It was 25ft long, with space for two divers sitting astride it. Its propeller was powered by a 2 horsepower electric motor, which could drive it underwater for up to six hours at 3 knots. It had ballast tanks and a trim motor, while the warhead consisted of a detachable 600lb charge of high explosives. Initial trials were a success, so Fell ordered a number of these Chariots to be built.

The Royal Navy now had its own answer to the Italian 'human torpedo'. The operation was moved up to Loch Cairnbawn in the north-east of Scotland, where a depot ship, the *Titania*, was anchored to provide a base for the continued training of the 'charioteers'. These culminated in a mock attack on the battleship *Howe*, which was well defended by anti-torpedo nets, boom defences, hydrophones, searchlights and patrol craft. Despite this, three Chariots penetrated her defences undetected and laid their

The small Norwegian-built fishing boat *Arthur* formed part of 'The Shetland Bus', ferrying agents, information and equipment between Shetland and Norway. During Operation *Title* – the attempted attack on *Tirpitz* in the Faettenfjord – it was used to transport two Chariots, 'human torpedoes', to Norway. The attempt failed, and the *Arthur* was scuttled, leaving her crew and the charioteers to try to make it across country to Sweden.

charges beneath the battleship. Three more, though, were forced to abandon the attack for various technical reasons, while another was spotted by the defenders after laying her charges. The exercise was repeated the following evening, with similar results. If the attack had been real, the *Howe* would have been sunk. The Chariots and their crews were ready for the real thing. All they needed was a way of reaching the *Tirpitz* in the Faettenfjord.

Operation *Title*

The means were provided by a Norwegian naval officer named Leif Larsen. Having escaped from German-occupied Norway, he became involved in 'The Shetland Bus', a clandestine operation which maintained a link between Britain and resistance cells in Norway. Larsen commanded one of the fishing boats used to sustain this maritime link, which operated between Scalloway in Shetland and the Norwegian coast near Bergen, transporting agents, equipment and information across the North Sea. In the summer of 1942, Larsen flew to London for talks with naval intelligence officers, and from there a plan was developed which would involve using 'The Shetland Bus' to transport Chariots to the Faettenfjord. Larsen set about modifying his fishing boat, the *Arthur*, so it could carry two Chariots attached to the underside of her hull. The derrick was strengthened, and a secret compartment installed, so the charioteers could hide if the vessel was stopped and searched by a German patrol.

Trials were then carried out off Loch Cairnbawn, and a mock attack was carried out on the battleship *Rodney*, which proved a resounding success. False papers were produced for the ship and crew, and for the charioteers, who were expected to make their way home by way of neutral Sweden after the attack. Finally, on 26 October, the *Arthur* set off from Scalloway, waved off from the jetty by Commander Fell. The little fishing boat had a rough time of it crossing the North Sea, but landfall was made at noon on 28 October. Despite a worrying mechanical breakdown, they then motored up the coast under cover of darkness, and entered the fjord near the small island of Edøya, posing as a coastal freighter transporting peat from Edøya to Trondheim. They were still plagued by engine trouble, and had to put in to a fishing village for minor repairs. However, this was soon fixed and their journey was resumed.

Shortly afterwards they were stopped by a German patrol boat, but allowed to continue on their way. Then, at around 5pm on 31 October, as they were nearing Trondheim, the crew heard knocking from beneath the hull. One of the Chariots was working itself loose in the rapidly deteriorating weather. They couldn't do anything about it, as they were too close to the port. The weather deteriorated, and at 10pm there was a loud grinding noise. The *Arthur* put in to a sheltered bay, and one of the charioteers went over the side to have a look. Moments later he surfaced, reporting that the Chariots had gone – they'd broken loose in the storm. At that point they were just 10 miles from the *Tirpitz*, lying unsuspectingly in the Faettenfjord. If that storm hadn't sprung up then the course of the naval war might well have been altered. However, with the Chariots lost, the mission had ended in failure.

Larsen steamed past the entrance to the battleship's lair, and at 1am on 1 November he scuttled the *Arthur* in the Trondheimsfjord, and her crew and the charioteers rowed ashore. They made their way to the Swedish frontier, while the *Arthur* drifted inshore a little as she sank, coming to rest with her masts sticking out above the water of the fjord. The Germans raised the fishing boat, discovered the secret compartments and figured out what had happened. However, by then Larsen and his companions had reached the border. There, a surprise encounter with a two-man German police patrol ended with the policemen being killed, and Bob Evans, one of the charioteers, seriously wounded. He had to be left behind, while the rest managed to escape into Sweden. Evans survived, only to be captured, interrogated and then shot as a spy. It was a dismal end to what had been a very well-conceived and monumentally courageous operation.

The X-craft

This would prove to be the last attack on *Tirpitz* in her lair near Trondheim. Her crew spent the winter carrying out maintenance on the battleship, as it was deemed too dangerous to send her south to a harbour in Germany. After a period of exercises and trials she was ready for operational duties again. Finally, in March 1943, *Tirpitz* moved north, first to Bogen near Narvik and then to the Altenfjord near North Cape. By 23 March she had dropped anchor in her new lair, the Kaafjord, an easterly spur of the much larger Altenfjord. It was there that the ship would remain throughout the summer, within easy reach of the Arctic Convoys. As this new forward base was almost 900 nautical miles from Shetland, a repeat of Operation *Title* was out of the question. A new means had to be found to attack the German

There was very little space inside the control room of an X-craft. The boat's commander, the second-in-command and the engineer were stationed here during an attack. The fourth crew member, the diver, was stationed in the W&D compartment just forward of the control room.

battleship. Fortuitously for the British, the Royal Navy now had the means to carry out such a long-distance attack.

Back in June 1940, when Major Jefferis had been seconded to the Navy's Department of Naval Construction (DNC), work began on designing a midget submarine capable of carrying out attacks of this sort. Jefferis first produced the Admiralty's 'staff requirement' for the craft – a combination of its specifications and its purpose. It would be a submarine in miniature, with a crew of three or four men, capable of operating where larger submarines were unable to go. That especially meant that it could operate submerged in shallow or confined waters. It would be able to lay magnetic mines or some other type of charge, and would have a submerged range of around 80 nautical miles, operating at about 4 knots. During 1941 a design was produced, under the guidance of Cromwell Varley, now the owner of the Varley Marine Works outside Southampton. He in turn was assisted by Commander T. I. S. 'Tizzy' Bell, who would supervise the training of the craft's crew.

At the time, the naval dockyards were working flat-out to repair damaged warships and build new ones. The DNC thus decided to allocate the building of its first prototype midget submarine to a private shipyard. Naturally enough, Varley's own company was selected. Work on what became known as 'Job 82' began at Varley Marine, where the design was modified and refined as the prototype took shape. Varley used full-sized

The dive control position on an X-craft, which was normally occupied by the boat's second-in-command. The hydroplane, ballast pump and main motor controls could be operated from this position, just aft of the seat occupied by the boat's commander.

wooden mock-ups to test the layout of the craft, to make sure everything fitted together in a logical way. This small submersible, the first X-craft, was officially designated *X-3*. There had already been an *X-1* and an *X-2* in the submarine service – the latter being an Italian boat captured in 1940. Work also began on a second slightly larger prototype, *X-4*, in HM Dockyard in Portsmouth. Work on the two craft continued during the winter of 1941/42, until finally, on 19 March 1942, *X-3* was launched on the River Hamble.

Superficially, these X-craft resembled the early Holland submarines of the early 1900s. They were small and rode low in the water, with a slightly raised casemate rather than a conning tower. *X-3* was 43ft 6in long, with a beam of just 5ft 6in, and a displacement of 24 tons. It had a maximum diving depth of 200ft, while its Gardner diesel engine, taken from a London bus, gave it a speed of 6 knots on the surface. Once submerged, its batteries

The engine of *X-24*. The boat was powered by a Gardner diesel engine of exactly the same kind as was fitted to wartime London buses, as well as a small but powerful electric motor for use when the craft was submerged. For display purposes *X-24* has been cut in two, at the bulkhead between the control room and the engine compartment. This shows the interior of the engine and steering compartment, looking aft. (Photograph by Eachan Hardie)

would propel it at 5 knots. Rising above its coaming was an attack periscope, a navigation periscope and an induction mast – a form of snorkel – while the stern was dominated by a single propeller, flanked by a two-part rudder and a hydroplane. On top of the coaming were two hatches – one aft of the attack periscope, the other forward of the induction mast.

Other midget submarines were produced during the war, by the Germans, the Japanese and the Italians. However, it was this second hatch which set the X-craft apart. It led to a 'Wet & Dry (W&D) Compartment', an airlock chamber which divided the submersible in two. Forward of it lay the battery compartments and stowage areas, while aft of it was the main control room, with the engine compartment behind it. The W&D compartment was designed to be sealed from the rest of the boat, and it could then be flooded. A diver inside the W&D compartment could then make his way out of the X-craft by way of the W&D hatch, cut anti-torpedo nets, lay charges or do any other tasks a diver might be required to perform, and then return to the boat. The water would then be pumped out. This gave the X-craft a great degree of flexibility, particularly if the crew encountered any snags while carrying out their mission.

The X-craft wasn't designed to carry torpedoes, like a more conventional submarine. Instead, a pair of side charges were bolted to its flanks. Effectively these were mines, albeit streamlined ones, which conformed to the shape of the craft's hull. Each weighed 4 tons, and contained 2 tons of Amatex high explosives. This was an extremely sensitive form of chemical explosive, combining RDX and TNT with ammonium nitrate. It was detonated by means of a clock timer, linked to a fuse. The idea was that the crew would release the side charges underneath their target, or at least close by it, and then withdraw from the area as the clock counted down. The charge was deemed sufficient to sink most warships, or, in the case of battleships like *Tirpitz*, at least damage them so extensively that they would no longer pose a threat.

While the first two X-craft were transported to Faslane in Scotland, where their crews would familiarize themselves with their boats, in July the Admiralty ordered that six more X-craft would be produced, albeit modified slightly in light of lessons learned from the sea trials of the prototypes. This time Vickers-Armstrong were given the contract, so *X-5* to *X-10* would be built in their yard in Barrow-in-Furness. For these, the DNC demanded that they incorporate a slightly stronger pressure hull, allowing them to dive to 300ft, and that they carry better Exide batteries, giving them a greater range when submerged. These full production X-craft would also be fitted with a high-quality gyro-compass, hydrophones to detect enemy ships, and a target indicator device to reduce the chances of being detected underwater.

A young submarine officer using the main attack periscope of an X-craft. This was normally the position of the boat's commander, within sight of the gyro-compass. During Operation *Source*, both the periscope and the gyro-compass developed problems, which severely handicapped the X-craft crews.

The only real drawback of the X-craft design was that it was extremely cramped. Each boat had a four-man crew. The craft's commander was assisted by another officer, a qualified diver and an Engine Room Artificer. These four men had to stay confined in this small space for several days at a time. One X-craft commander described it as a bit like living inside a railway steam engine's boiler. Nobody could stand fully upright inside one of them, and the limited bunk space meant that the crew would have to take turns to lie down and sleep. Sanitation and cooking facilities were minimal, and the crew had to negotiate a mass of pipes, air bottles, batteries, gauges and valves. The same former commander compared being given command of an X-craft with being given a toy train set for Christmas, as it was like a real submarine, only in miniature.

Crew training on Loch Striven, summer 1943 (overleaf)

On 15 March 1942 the prototype *X-3* was launched on the River Hamble, near Southampton. In late August, once her sea trials were complete, the craft was transported north to Scotland. The new base for the midget submarine programme would be HMS *Varbel* on the Isle of Bute, but the main operational area for crew training would be Loch Striven, a few miles to the north-west. Ardtaraig House at the head of the sea loch became a forward base for the squadron, and was duly renamed *Varbel II*. Training of midget submarine crews continued throughout the late summer and autumn, and in January 1943 the first of the fully operational X-craft appeared. Then crew training began in earnest. This was a hard, exhausting, but thorough process, so that by the late summer of 1943 there were enough highly trained and motivated submariners available in the flotilla that the six boats could double up on crews. This meant the planners could use a passage crew to help transport the X-craft to Norwegian waters, and a second operational crew to actually carry out the attack. Here, during the early summer of 1943, the crew of an X-craft can be seen practicing the change-over of crews while heaved to in the sea loch. At this stage many modifications were being tried out. On this boat, *X-10*, a safety support known as the Hezlet rail has been added to the induction mast.

During the second half of 1942 the crews of the prototypes learned on the job, operating from a shore base called HMS *Varbel* on the Isle of Bute, named after Commanders Varley and Bell. The initial wave of submariners there were soon joined by others. Support ships were assigned to the force, and the sea trials and crew training gave way to operational training exercises – preparing for the real thing. Other boats would arrive too, until the last of the six Vickers boats, *X-10*, arrived in Faslane in January 1943. That was when the X-craft flotilla really came into its own. With these new boats, it now had the craft it needed to attack targets like the *Tirpitz*. Once the crews were thoroughly familiar with their strange little craft, and a suitable plan was devised, then the X-craft could be unleashed against the *Tirpitz*.

Preparing for Operation *Source*

X-3 was commanded by Lieutenant Donald Cameron RNR, a former merchant naval officer, who joined the Royal Navy at the outbreak of war. It was Cameron who conducted the sea trials on the River Hamble, and who advised the designers on the modifications needed for the new batch of craft. He was an expert seaman, and a thoroughly accomplished submariner who could be relied upon, whatever the circumstances. *X-4*'s commander was Sub-Lieutenant Godfrey Place RN, one of the few regulars in the flotilla. He was just 22, but already showed promise as a highly proficient and gifted submariner. The two crews trained in nearby Loch Striven, and a second forward base was established in Ardtaraig House, a shooting lodge at the head of the narrow sea loch: it was duly named *Varbel II*.

The crew of a later X-craft, *X-21*, during training in Loch Striven, on the west coast of Scotland during the autumn of 1944. On the left is Lieutenant John Terry-Lloyd, who commanded the passage crew of *X-5* during Operation *Source*. The open hatch leads to the boat's W&D compartment.

They had accidents – in early November 1942 *X-3* was lost during a training dive in Loch Striven, but Lieutenant Lorimer and his two-man crew managed to escape. The X-craft was eventually raised, and sent back to Gosport to be repaired and refitted. The following month Place's *X-4* had a fatal accident, as a young officer, Sub-Lieutenant Morgan Thomas, was lost overboard in rough weather and drowned. The waves also swamped the W&D compartment, leaving the two remaining men inside trapped for two hours, with the craft tipped bows-down. Then on 31 May Sub-Lieutenant David Locke drowned while practicing net cutting outside *X-7*, the victim of a breathing problem with his re-breather set. Given the experimental nature of

An X-craft photographed at the moment she commenced to dive during a crew training exercise in Loch Striven. Her periscope has been fully extended, so she will be running submerged just below the surface of the sea loch. Unlike a conventional submarine, an X-craft could also dive vertically, without using her dive planes.

the boats, it was surprising there weren't more fatalities. Some asked to return to regular duties, or were transferred, but those who remained were fast becoming experts in their strange craft and their capabilities.

In January 1943 the training regime picked up its pace as the first of the Vickers boats began to arrive at *Varbel*. As more crews and men arrived, the emphasis changed, from training the men and learning the ways of the X-craft, to practicing for 'the real thing'. By then the force had a name – the 12th Submarine Flotilla, under the command of Captain William 'Willy' Banks. Officially its base was *Varbel*, the former hotel overlooking Port Bannatyne in Bute. It was there, over drinks, that the crews discussed tactics and debated the latest rumours about when or where they might make their first attack. A depot ship, the *Bonaventure*, was attached to the flotilla, with the facilities to lift the X-craft out of the water and service them or prepare them for their mission. By the spring of 1943 the training of the crews had reached its peak, and it was clear to the Admiralty that the flotilla was ready for action. Plans began to be drawn up which would culminate in Operation *Source* – the attack on the *Tirpitz*.

The men of the flotilla weren't stupid – they knew *Tirpitz* would be their most likely target. Like the Admiralty's planners, they realized that an attack during the summer was unlikely, as the longer hours of daylight made the enterprise too hazardous. When it was clear that the flotilla wouldn't be fully operational before the end of April, it was obvious that any attack would most likely take place in the autumn. Meanwhile, the two fatalities led to improvements. First, a safety rail – the Hezlet rail – was installed in the boats to reduce the chances of a crewman being lost overboard.

A later midget submarine, *X-25*, which differed slightly from the earlier type used in Operation *Source*. What is visible here, above and behind her commander Lieutenant Smart, is a 'Hezlet rail', a safety bar and strap attached to the raised engine room induction mast. Another post-*Source* innovation was the small bar at the front of the casing, to prevent it from snagging on an anti-torpedo net.

Improvements were then made to the diver's equipment, and a safer method was found to cut through anti-torpedo nets. The latter involved cooperation between the diver and the commander, who was watching for the diver's hand signals through his periscope; the diver would literally guide the X-craft through the hole he'd just cut.

By July 1943 it was clear that an operation was imminent. The flotilla left its base on Bute, and moved to Loch Cairnbawn. *Bonaventure* (or 'BV' as she was affectionately known) would serve as the flotilla's base there. The training continued, with the emphasis on net-cutting and charge-laying. The crews were reaching a peak of efficiency and morale was extremely high. Meanwhile, the planners were making their final preparations. Originally, the operation was planned in secret by the staff of Flag Officer Submarines, based in Gosport, but they drew on the suggestions and expertise of the flotilla too. The planners faced a number of problems, the largest of which was the means of getting the X-craft to the north of Norway. Then there were the defences of the Altenfjord and Kaafjord to consider, as well as those surrounding the battleship itself. To help provide this information, Photograph Reconnaissance Unit (PRU) flights were undertaken from air bases in the Soviet Union, while some help was also provided by the Red Air Force.

As for the problem of distance, it was a little over 1,000 nautical miles from Loch Cairnbawn at the head of Eddrachillis Bay to the mouth of the Altenfjord. While the X-craft could theoretically make the voyage, it would be an impossible strain on the men's endurance. They could be loaded onto a surface ship such as the *Bonaventure*, and winched into the sea off their destination, but that ran too high a risk of being spotted by German U-boats, surface patrols or aircraft. Not only would that invite an attack on the 'mother ship', but it would warn the Germans that an attack was imminent. It was decided that each X-craft would be towed to Norway by another submarine; that way both boats could dive to avoid being detected. That decision made, it was just a matter of planning the logistics of the towing operation.

X-5 being towed out of Loch Cairnbawn by HMS *Thrasher* at the start of Operation *Source*. Her commander during the passage was Lieutenant Terry-Lloyd, a South African, who can be seen peering out of the boat's main hatch. The towing submarine used a nylon rope, which was much stronger than the manila ropes used to tow *X-7*, *X-8* and *X-9*. The towing problems experienced during the passage were limited to those X-craft using the inferior man-made tow ropes.

Even then, it was felt that the passage would place a lot of strain on the crews. Two crews would therefore be used – a 'passage crew' to man the X-craft during the journey to the Altenfjord, and then an 'operational crew', who would man the craft during the mission itself. During the passage to Norway, the operational crew would be carried on board the 'mother' submarine, and would be encouraged to rest as much as they could during the voyage. With that problem sorted out, the planners then considered the date of the operation. They wanted some moonlight, to allow the crews to navigate the Altenfjord and find the target, but not enough to increase the chances of detection. It also had to be some time after mid-September, when the nights were considered long enough to give the operation a reasonable chance of success. During 20–25 September 1943 the moon would be waning, and in its last quarter: 20 September was seen as the optimum date for the X-craft to be released off the Altenfjord.

It was decided that *Tirpitz* wouldn't be the only target. The whole German naval group in the area tended to remain together, but occasionally warships would leave the fjord to conduct gunnery exercises or other similar missions. There was even the possibility that the warships wouldn't be in the Kaafjord at all, but would move to one of their other known locations – the Bodenfjord near Narvik or the Faettenfjord near Trondheim. Plans were developed for attacks on all three of these anchorages. For planning purposes, they were codenamed *Funnel*, *Empire* and *Forced* respectively. The actual mission, whichever one would be implemented, was codenamed

HMS *Bonaventure* in Loch Cairnbawn, with the submarine depot ship HMS *Titania* anchored in the background, shortly before the commencement of Operation *Source*. A pair of towing submarines can be seen lying off *Titania's* starboard side, with more off her port beam. This sea loch served as the launching point for the mission.

Operation *Source*. While *Tirpitz* would be the midget submarines' principal target, the intention was also to attack two other targets in the same anchorage – the battlecruiser *Scharnhorst* and armoured cruiser *Lützow*.

During the passage, PRU flights and reports from the Norwegian Resistance would be passed to Gosport by way of the Admiralty, giving updates on any ship movements. These would then be passed to the 'mother' submarines so that the operational crews would know what to expect when they reached the Kaafjord. Even this was a major undertaking. PRU Spitfires from 543 Squadron were transported to northern Russia and based in Vaenga near Murmansk. They would fly these last-minute photo reconnaissance missions. Then either a series of Mosquitoes would be used to transport the photos to Britain by flying over the Baltic, or else a Catalina would fly them over the Arctic Sea. The Norwegian Resistance in the area were prepared to send in sighting reports of any German ship movements or unusual activity. One of these agents, Torstein Raaby, was particularly well placed, as he lived almost within sight of the German anchorage.

After the X-craft were released from the 'mother' submarine, each boat was on its own. They had no means of keeping in contact with each other, let alone the 'mother' boats. After the departure of their charges, the 'mother' submarines would patrol an assigned sector off the Søroy Strait, at the mouth of the Altenfjord, while avoiding known minefields in the area. They would then wait for their X-craft to return. After the attack, the X-craft would attempt to rendezvous with them, but if all else failed a fallback rendezvous was established in a deserted bay off the northern end

A later X-craft on the surface, with the boat's commander standing on the coaming by the engine room intake mast. A mouthpiece there allowed him to give orders directly to the helmsman. This craft is *X-21*, commanded by Lieutenant Terry-Lloyd, who commanded the passage crew of *X-5* during Operation *Source*.

of the island of Søroy. As a last resort the crews would make their own way to Murmansk.

The idea was to release the X-craft at dusk on 20 September, allowing the midget submarines to make their way through the minefields while there was still enough light to detect any mines. During the daylight hours of 21 September they would lie submerged in the Altenfjord, getting under way again after dark. It was expected that they would reach the entrance to the Kaafjord at dawn on 22 September, when they would make their attack.

The passage and operational crews of *X-9*. Back (left to right): Lieutenant Martin, Lieutenant Shean, Sub-Lieutenant Brooks, Sub-Lieutenant Kearon. Front (left to right): Able Seaman Harte, ER Artificer Coles, Stoker Hollett. Kearon, Harte and Hollett were lost when *X-9* foundered.

Lieutenant Henry Henty-Creer RNVR (right) and another young officer, pictured on board the support vessel *Bonaventure* while anchored in Loch Striven in 1943. The Australian-born Henty-Creer was just 23 when he and his crew were lost in action during the attack on the *Tirpitz*.

This is what they'd been training for with such care – penetrating the enemy's anti-torpedo defences and protective booms, and laying their charges underneath their target. It was decided that six X-craft would take part in the operation – all of them the new ones built by Vickers in Barrow. *X-5*, *X-6* and *X-7* would attack the *Tirpitz*, *X-8* would target the *Lützow*, while *X-9* and *X-10* would go for the *Scharnhorst*. The latest reports placed all three German warships in the Kaafjord, within sight of each other.

On 30 August the submarine depot ship *Titania* arrived in Loch Cairnbawn to support the submarines which would be used as the 'mother' boats for the 12th Flotilla. The six submarines themselves appeared over the next few days. The two Triton-class (or T-class) boats *Thrasher* and *Truculent* were joined by four Improved S-class boats – *Sea Nymph*, *Sceptre*, *Stubborn* and *Syrtis*. Each of them was allocated an X-craft to tow into Arctic waters. On 1 September all leave was cancelled and a security clampdown imposed: no vessels could enter or leave the loch. Then, on board *Bonaventure*, all the commanders were given a full briefing by Commander G. P. S. Davies RN, the officer who had supervised the planning of the operation on behalf of Flag Officer Submarines. Davies outlined the plan, then went through its fine detail. During this briefing, men were allocated to be either passage or operational crews. Some were disappointed, but everyone was enthused by the importance of their mission.

Meanwhile, towing practices were carried out, while everyone saw to all the last-minute preparations that could make a difference between success or failure. The day the operation would begin was set for Saturday, 11 September. Three days before, the whole force of men and boats were inspected by Rear Admiral Sir Claud Barry, Flag Officer Submarines, who had succeeded Admiral Horton the previous November. Barry was impressed, describing the X-craft crews as being like boys on the last day of term. He added that their confidence wasn't due to daredevilry, but rather to 'the firm conviction, formed during many months of arduous training, that their submarines were capable of doing all that their crews demanded of them, and the crews were quite capable of surmounting any difficulties or hazards which it was possible for human beings to conquer'. With the Flag Officer's final approval and blessing, the daring mission could finally get under way.

THE RAID

The passage

The six submarines had all been specially fitted with towing brackets at their stern, as had two more, *Satyr* and *Sea Dog*, which were waiting in Scapa Flow in case they were needed. The X-craft had also all been taken on board the *Bonaventure* to have their side charges fitted. After a final round of towing practice, and the transfer of crews from submarine to X-craft, everything was ready. After nearly 18 months of training and preparation, the Royal Navy's midget submarine force was about to go into action. The night before, Rear Admiral Barry threw a lively dinner for the commanders of the passage and operational crews. The following morning, while some nursed their sore heads, others quietly settled their affairs, wrote home or made other last-minute preparations. Then, at 4pm on 11 September, the submarine *Truculent* headed out towards the open sea, with *X-6* in tow. They were followed by five more pairings – *Thrasher* and *X-5*, *Stubborn* and *X-7*, *Sea Nymph* and *X-8*, *Syrtis* with *X-9* and *Sceptre* with *X-10*.

Rear Admiral Barry waved them off, and in reply the commander of *Syrtis* blared an old car horn. It was a happy, optimistic departure, but Lieutenant Cameron on the bridge of *Truculent* couldn't help looking at the coast of his native Scotland receding, and wondering if he would ever see it again. They made 8–10 knots while they headed north towards Cape Wrath, the north-westerly tip of the Scottish mainland. Shortly after leaving Eddrachillis Bay, the X-craft dived down to 50ft to reduce the effect of the surface swell. The weather was good, but once in open water they experienced 'porpoising': once the midget submarine was submerged, thanks to the jerking of the towing cable it could rear up and down in the water by as much as 60ft. This meant the crew had to constantly adjust their depth. It was an exhausting business.

Apart from that, at that stage the passage was reasonably uneventful. The only incident that night was when an armed trawler off Orkney almost

The passage and operational crews of *X-5*. Back (left to right): Lieutenant Terry-Lloyd, Sub-Lieutenant Malcolm, Lieutenant Henty-Creer, Sub-Lieutenant Nelson. Front (left to right): Stoker Garrity, Acting Leading Seaman Element, ER Artificer Mortiboys. Henty-Creer, Malcolm, Nelson and Mortiboys lost their lives in *X-5* when she was sunk in the Kaafjord.

rammed and sank *X-6*, which had just surfaced to replenish its air and recharge the batteries. Disaster was narrowly averted, and the passage continued. Slowly, a routine was established. The X-craft would surface every six hours, as *X-6* had done, but otherwise the small craft would remain submerged, with two men on watch and one man off throughout the passage. Those on watch had to keep a constant eye on the depth gauge and inclinometer in case something untoward happened. They also had to keep an eye on the towing submarine through the attack periscope, in case they flashed an urgent signal.

The rest of the time the passage crew maintained the boat, took readings of fuel and battery level and diesel oil pressure, checked the electrical circuits and generally kept the craft in shape. They also kept an ear out for any sounds that might suggest a problem with the tow line. The only relief came when the towing submarine signalled that it was okay to surface. Then came the lengthy business of recharging air bottles and batteries, and replacing stale air with fresh: submariners called this process 'guffing through'. The newer T-class boats could maintain a speed of 10 knots, but the older S-class boats only made 8.5 knots. Still, the tow continued, every hour taking the X-craft closer to their targets.

***Operation Source* crews**

X-craft	Passage crew	Operational crew
X-5	Lt Terry-Lloyd L. Seaman Element Stoker (1st Class) Garrity	Lt Henty-Creer Sub-Lt Malcolm Sub-Lt Nelson ER Artificer Mortiboys
X-6	Lt Wilson L. Seaman McGregor Stoker (1st Class) Oakley	Lt Cameron Sub-Lt Lorimer Sub-Lt Kendall ER Artificer Goddard
X-7	Lt Philip Able Seaman Magennis Stoker (1st Class) Luck	Lt Place Sub-Lt Whittam Sub-Lt Aitken ER Artificer Whitley
X-8	Lt Smart L. Seaman Pomeroy Stoker (1st Class) Robinson	Lt McFarlane Lt Marsden Sub-Lt Hindmarsh ER Artificer Murray
X-9	Sub-Lt Kearon Able Seaman Harte Stoker Hollett	Lt Martin Sub-Lt Brooks Lt Shean ER Artificer Coles
X-10	Sub-Lt Page Petty Officer Brookes ER Artificer Fishleigh	Lt Hudspeth Sub-Lt Enzer Sub-Lt Harding ER Artificer Tilley

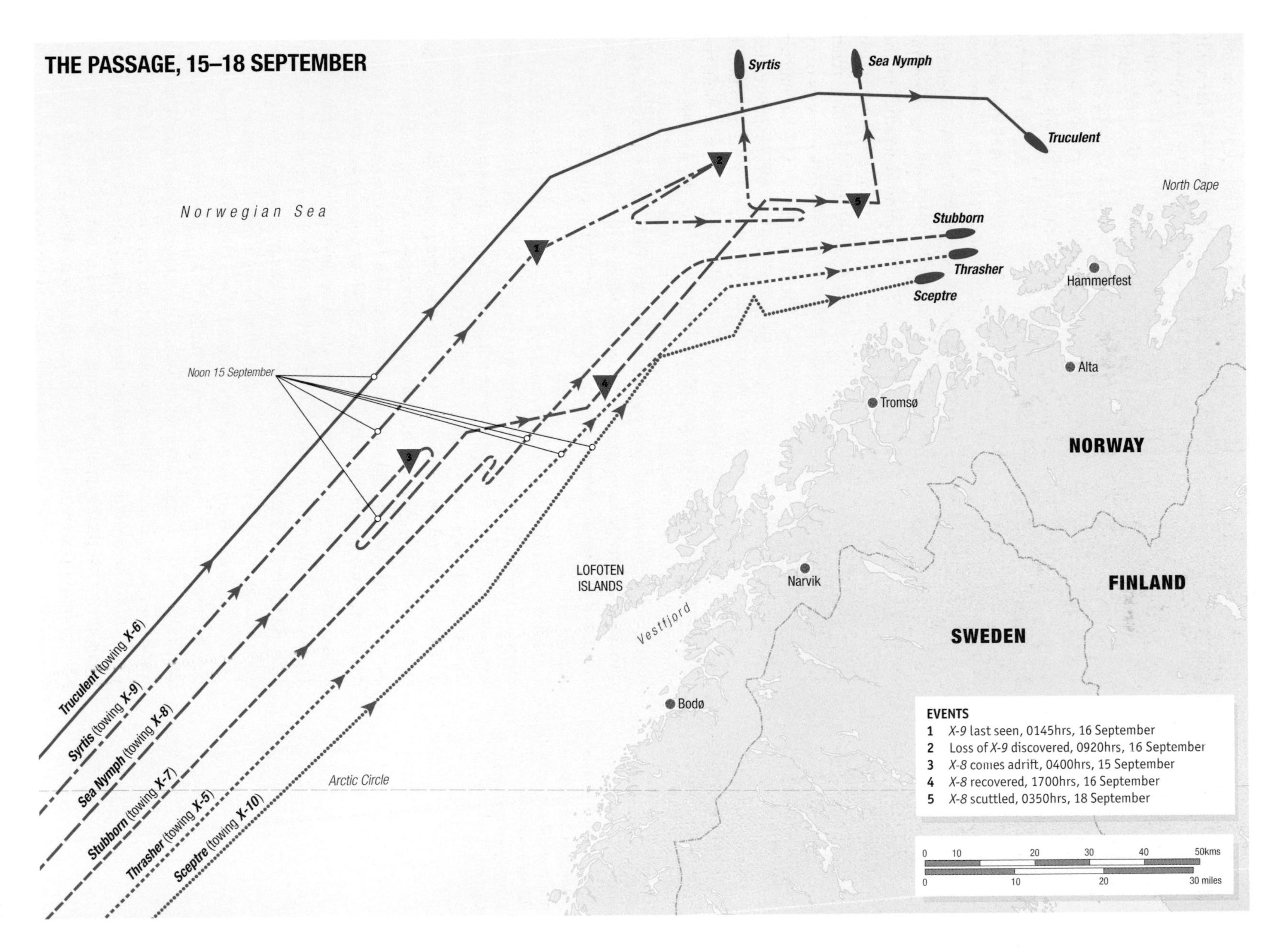
THE PASSAGE, 15–18 SEPTEMBER
Syrtis
Sea Nymph
Truculent
North Cape
Norwegian Sea
Stubborn
Thrasher
Sceptre
Hammerfest
Alta
Tromsø
Noon 15 September
NORWAY
LOFOTEN ISLANDS
Narvik
FINLAND
Vestfjord
SWEDEN
Bodø
Truculent (towing X-6)
Syrtis (towing X-9)
Sea Nymph (towing X-8)
Stubborn (towing X-7)
Thrasher (towing X-5)
Sceptre (towing X-10)
Arctic Circle
EVENTS
1 X-9 last seen, 0145hrs, 16 September
2 Loss of X-9 discovered, 0920hrs, 16 September
3 X-8 comes adrift, 0400hrs, 15 September
4 X-8 recovered, 1700hrs, 16 September
5 X-8 scuttled, 0350hrs, 18 September
0 10 20 30 40 50kms
0 10 20 30 miles

The passage and operational crews of *X-7*. Back (left to right): Sub-Lieutenant Aitken, Lieutenant Place, Sub-Lieutenant Whittam, Lieutenant Philip. Front (left to right): Able Seaman Magennis, Stoker Luck, ER Artificer Whitley. Whittam and Whitley lost their lives when *X-7* foundered in the Kaafjord.

Meanwhile, on the towing submarines, the passage crews rested, or else got together to go over their mission. They had been promised updates on what was going on in the Kaafjord, and these were radioed to the towing submarines on the evening of Thursday, 16 September – five days into the voyage. There had been a brief panic, as on 6 September *Tirpitz*, *Scharnhorst* and nine destroyers left the Kaafjord, heading north. This was an exercise which the Germans codenamed Operation *Sizilien* (Sicilian) – a bombardment of the Free Norwegian outpost on Spitzbergen. On 8 September the capital ships fired on these shore installations, and then landing parties were sent ashore to round up prisoners. The force then returned to the Kaafjord. Similarly, *Lützow* was away for parts of the month, its crew conducting gunnery exercises.

Sizilien was little more than a glorified form of target practice, a morale-booster, but for a while it worried the Admiralty, who feared that the X-craft would be attacking an empty anchorage. Rear Admiral Barry almost postponed the whole enterprise. However, the two German capital ships returned to their lair, and Operation *Source* proceeded as planned. The British submariners were relieved that the latest PRU flights had reported that the *Tirpitz*, *Scharnhorst* and *Lützow* were still at anchor, with the armoured cruiser berthed in the Langefjord, another offshoot of the larger Altenfjord.

Shortly after midnight on Wednesday, 15 September, four days into the mission, the weather began to deteriorate. The first sign of trouble came from the *X-8* when the underwater telephone cable running along its tow rope stopped working. The crew of the *Sea Nymph* were unable to repair it due to the rough seas. Then at 4am the tow line parted. Nobody on the towing submarine noticed this for two hours, when the X-craft was due to surface to recharge her air and batteries. The boat's navigator checked the chart, and reported that they had travelled 36 miles since *X-8* had last dived, some six hours before. So, she could be anywhere along that track. The submarine's commander, Lt John Oakley, turned the boat around and increased speed. Extra lookouts were posted, but by noon, having combed the whole area, the boat's log reported that no sighting had been made.

In fact, it was *Stubborn* which spotted *X-8*. They had just dived after sighting a possible U-boat, but it was actually the *X-8*. They spotted her again after resurfacing, as did the crew of *X-7*, being towed behind *Stubborn*. The *Stubborn*'s commander, Lieutenant Arthur Duff, ordered Lieutenant Jack Smart of *X-8* to head north, guiding him towards the *Sea Nymph*. However, Smart misheard the order in the wind, and steered the wrong course. Now two submarines were looking for the missing boat. It was finally located at 5pm on 16 September. Smart and his passage crew were now exhausted, so

The passage and operational crews of *X-8*. Back (left to right): Sub-Lieutenant Hindmarsh, Lieutenant McFarlane, Lieutenant Smart, Lieutenant Marsden. Front (left to right): ER Artificer Murray, Stoker Robinson, Leading Seaman Pomeroy.

on the *Sea Nymph*, Lieutenant Brian 'Digger' McFarlane, commanding the operational crew, decided to relieve Smart and his men. Once *X-8* was under tow again, and the passage crew relieved, *Sea Nymph* resumed her passage to the Altenfjord.

Earlier that morning, disaster had overtaken *X-9* and her crew. Everything had been going well until the early hours of 16 September. She had come up to 'guff', and at 1.20am the midget submarine dived again. The submarine *Syrtis* continued to tow the X-craft, which was supposedly maintaining a depth of 50ft. She made a steady 8½ knots throughout the night, and at 8.55am she reduced speed again, as *X-9* was due to surface. The signal that it was safe to come up was the dropping of small underwater explosive charges – a bit like hand grenades. The crew of *Syrtis* waited, but nothing happened. Then someone noticed that the towing cable was trailing limply behind them. It seemed that it had parted during the night. The commander of *Syrtis*, Lieutenant Jupp, turned his boat around and steered a reciprocal course – heading back the way he had come.

It was a simple job to calculate that since *X-9* was last sighted at 1.20am, the craft could be anywhere along the 65 miles of ocean which *Syrtis* had travelled during the night. The search went on throughout the day, but it became increasingly clear that *X-9* and her three-man crew had vanished. At 5.45pm lookouts on the submarine spotted a small but well-defined oil slick, which extended in a line along the submarine's old track. Still, Jupp continued the search until early on Friday, 17 September, with no avail. The obvious conclusion was that *X-9* had foundered.

An examination of the towing rope may have revealed the cause. It was made of strong manila fibre, which had parted close to the *Syrtis*. If she was 'porpoising', *X-9* could well have been weighted down by the bows, thanks to the heavy waterlogged cable attached to her. It was enough to drag the submarine downwards, and her crew would have been unable to bring *X-9* back onto a level trim. Sub-Lieutenant Kearon and his two crewmen, Able Seaman Harte and Stoker Hollett, were lost when their submarine reached her crush depth. There was nothing Jupp could do, apart from keep heading northwards to make the rendezvous off the entrance to the Altenfjord. At least there he and his embarked operations crew might be able to help with the rest of the operation. On the way, Jupp radioed the report of the loss to the Admiralty in London, but for some reason the signal never got through. The grim news only reached them when *Syrtis* returned to Scapa Flow. For the sake of morale, Jupp kept clear of the other submarines and

An S-class submarine of the type used to tow the X-craft from the north-west of Scotland to northern Norway. Six S-class and two T-class boats were used as towing boats during Operation *Source*.

boats gathering off the mouth of the Altenfjord. The remaining submariners would therefore carry on with their mission, unaware that three of their companions had already been lost.

That wasn't the last major blow during the passage. Early on the morning of 17 September, Lieutenant McFarlane and the three-man operational crew of *X-8* noticed that water was pouring into the empty ballast tank on their starboard side. The boat was taking on a heavy list, and there was a real risk she would capsize. The tank formed part of the starboard side charge, so McFarlane had no option but to release it. That left them with only one side charge. When he jettisoned it, McFarlane set it to 'safe', which meant it shouldn't explode. However, some 15 minutes later it went off a mile or so astern of them. The X-craft was tossed around by the underwater blast, and her crew knocked off their feet. Still, no harm seemed to be done, and the tow resumed. A few hours later, the same thing started happening with the port ballast tank. They tried trimming the boat, but it did no good. Obviously the blast had damaged the tank's seal. Once again, the safety of the boat and her crew were in jeopardy.

McFarlane had no choice. He had to jettison the tank, and with it his last remaining saddle charge. He released it just before 5pm, and this time he set the timer to two hours. He used the telephone attached to the mooring line to tell Lieutenant Oakley in *Sea Nymph* what he was doing. After dropping the saddle tank, the submarine towed the X-craft away at 8 knots. In theory they should have been 16 nautical miles away when the saddle tank was detonated. However, the charge went off prematurely, when they'd barely covered a quarter of that distance. The resulting shock waves from the enormous explosion rocked both boats, and the W&D compartment on *X-8* began to flood. Pipes sprang leaks too, and water began entering the boat.

X-8 was already toothless, as she'd lost her side charges. Now she was clearly not going to make it much further. McFarlane and his companions tried to repair the leaks, but to little avail, so he surfaced and signalled Oakley in the *Sea Nymph*. A rubber dingy was sent over to them, and the X-craft crew scrambled aboard after scuttling their boat. With both X-craft crews now embarked, *Sea Nymph* headed north towards her rendezvous. After all, she still had a job to do – helping to recover the remaining midget submarines after the raid. For McFarlane and his three crew, however, the mission was over. Of the six X-craft which had left Scotland, only four were now left.

Later that day – Friday, 17 September – the two faster T-class submarines *Thrasher* and *Truculent* made their landfall off Søroy Island, the entrance to the Altenfjord. Their passage had been uneventful, although nonetheless exhausting for the two passage crews. *Stubborn* and *Sea Nymph* arrived early on 20 September. Just a few hours before, the crew of the *Stubborn* and her charge *X-7* had an encounter which could have led to the loss of both submersibles. At 1.05am on Monday, 20 September, lookouts in *Stubborn* spotted a loose sea mine floating close by their port bow. It drifted past the submarine, but then became entangled in the towing cable leading to *X-7*. The mine worked its way down the cable until it bumped against the midget submarine's bows.

The two X-craft crews had been changed over during the evening of 18 September, so the operational crew were now running the craft. Their own manila cable had parted just after the transfer, but unlike *Syrtis* and *X-9*, the problem was spotted right away, and after three hours a new towing cable was in place. Lieutenant Place and his three-man crew must have felt the worst was behind them. Then came the encounter with the mine. Sub-Lieutenant Whittam was on watch when the mine was spotted, and *Stubborn* flashed a warning using her signal lamp. He called down into the boat to bring up Lieutenant Place, who recognized the mine as a German one. The mine's broken mooring cable was entangled in their own towing cable. So, Place used his feet to fend the mine off the side of the X-craft while trying to untangle the mooring rope from the manila cable. It was a nerve-racking few minutes: if the mine had detonated it would have sunk *X-7* in an instant, and probably *Stubborn* as well.

Eventually, Place managed to untangle the two lines, and slowly, after some more fending off with his sea boots, using a crumpled horn of the

An encounter with a German mine, 20 September 1943 (overleaf)

By midnight on 19/20 September, *X-7* and her towing submarine HMS *Stubborn* were off the Norwegian coast, to the west of the entrance to the Altenfjord. The operational crew, commanded by Lieutenant Godfrey Place, were now manning the midget submarine. At 1.05am the lookout on the *Stubborn* spotted a drifting sea mine off the port quarter of their submarine. Bobbing in the swell, it passed astern of the boat, only to become lodged in the tow rope linking *Stubborn* to *X-7*. It then started drifting towards the midget submarine. Sub-Lieutenant Bill Whittam, on watch on the boat's casing, called down the hatch to Place, who hurried up to the casing. The two officers soon realized it was a German tethered mine, whose steel mooring cable had come loose. The cable was now entangled in their tow rope. Place lowered his legs over the bows of the X-craft and, guided by Whittam, used his feet to keep the mine from touching the boat. He then turned, and placing one foot on the mine he loosened its mooring cable until it was no longer entangled in the towing rope. The mine was fended off, but Place kept 'walking' it down the side of the X-craft until it safely passed astern of her. If contact had been made, the X-craft would have been blown to pieces, and *Stubborn* badly damaged. Disaster was averted and *X-7* was able to carry out her attack as planned.

mine as a lever, the mine passed the boat and drifted harmlessly away. The official report by Rear Admiral Barry said afterwards that it was Place's 'deft footwork' that saved the day. Afterwards, Place decided they should all go below and have a restorative tot of rum. The X-craft dived again and the tow resumed. They were now nearly at their 'slipping point' – the place where the towing cable would be released, or 'slipped', and the X-craft left to make its own way towards its target. Thanks to the parted cable, and the mine incident, *Stubborn* and *X-7* would be the last pair of boats to reach their designated slipping point.

The passage and operational crews of *X-10*. Back (left to right): Sub-Lieutenant Harding, Lieutenant Hudspeth, Sub-Lieutenant Enzer, Sub-Lieutenant Page. Front (left to right): ER Artificer Tilley, Acting Petty Officer Brooks, ER Artificer Fishleigh.

The plan had called for all of the X-craft to be released off the Altenfjord at dusk on 20 September. With the exception of *X-8* and *X-9*, this had been done. The towing submarines then took up station at prearranged locations off the mouth of the fjord and a little further down the coast. Their job done, their next task was to linger unobserved, staying submerged during the day. They would then be in place to collect their charges after the attack – assuming of course that any of them had survived the operation. Three of the X-craft – *X-5*, *X-6* and *X-10* – had reached their slipping points safely before dawn on 20 September. They and their towing submarines then submerged, to wait for dusk. Early that evening, *X-7* joined them, lying at periscope depth just out of sight of land, waiting for nightfall.

Through the fjord

That evening, between 6.30pm and 7pm, the waiting boats all surfaced and the X-craft slipped their towlines. *Stubborn* and *X-7* followed suit at 8pm. In *X-6*, Cameron felt a sense of relief. The mission proper was under way, and he and his crew were now free to do the job they'd been training for. In his log, he described himself as 'a little tin god in a little tin can'. They made the passage inshore on the surface, moving independently under cover of darkness. Cameron noted that the Northern Lights – the aurora borealis – were providing a wonderful display in the Arctic sky above him, helping cast some extra light over the dangerous waters they were now heading through. The four remaining X-craft – *X-5*, *X-6*, *X-7* and *X-10* – were now crossing the large German minefield off Søroy Island. They made the passage through it with two men on the combing, looking out for any drifting mines, or ones on or just under the surface.

The large contact mines were there to stop bigger ships, and generally were tethered well below the keels of the small X-craft. However, it was

The Kaafjord, from a high-level PRU flight, shortly before Operation *Source*. *Tirpitz* can be seen in the bottom left, inside the Barbrudalen anti-torpedo net enclosure, while the spit at the top of the photograph is Auskarnes, with the empty berth for *Scharnhorst* in its lee, and the square enclosure for *Lützow* – also empty – just below the tip of the spit.

a tense time, the danger of an accident still there. Eventually, all of the boats made it through the mined area safely, emerging off its southern edge shortly before dawn. Then the four boats submerged and carried on towards the fjord. At that point the island of Søroy lay off their port beam, while ahead lay the smaller island of Stjernoy. Another island, Seiland, was off their port bow. Between Søroy and the two other islands was Søroy Sound, which led northwards towards the open sea near North Cape. Its other entrance – the one the X-craft had passed through – was protected by the minefield.

The entrance to the fjord they were heading towards was called Stjernsund, the narrow channel to the south of Atjernoy, between it and the Norwegian mainland. They continued through it during the daylight hours of Tuesday, 21 September, and by nightfall they had reached the sound's eastern end, where it opened out into the Altenfjord proper. Place later recalled that the passage through the Stjernsund was uneventful: he described it as 'a quiet day ... with very pleasant weather indeed'. He made the transit through the sound at 90ft, coming up now and then to check his bearings using the boat's periscope. It was during one of these periodic sweeps of his surroundings that he spotted something. Some way to the north-east, off Aarøy Island, he saw what he thought was a large warship with at least two escorts – probably destroyers. They came up the Altenfjord and turned north, heading around the northern side of Stjernoy. The ship was too far away to make out clearly.

Place didn't know it at the time, but the ship he spotted was the *Scharnhorst*, heading into the Arctic Sea beyond North Cape to conduct gunnery practice. He wasn't equipped to attack an enemy warship on the move, so he disregarded it. However, the departure of *Scharnhorst* caused some consternation in the Admiralty. Later that evening, a PRU reconnaissance flight did show that the *Scharnhorst* was no longer in the fjord. Nor was the *Lützow*. Both had mysteriously vanished during the night. Both

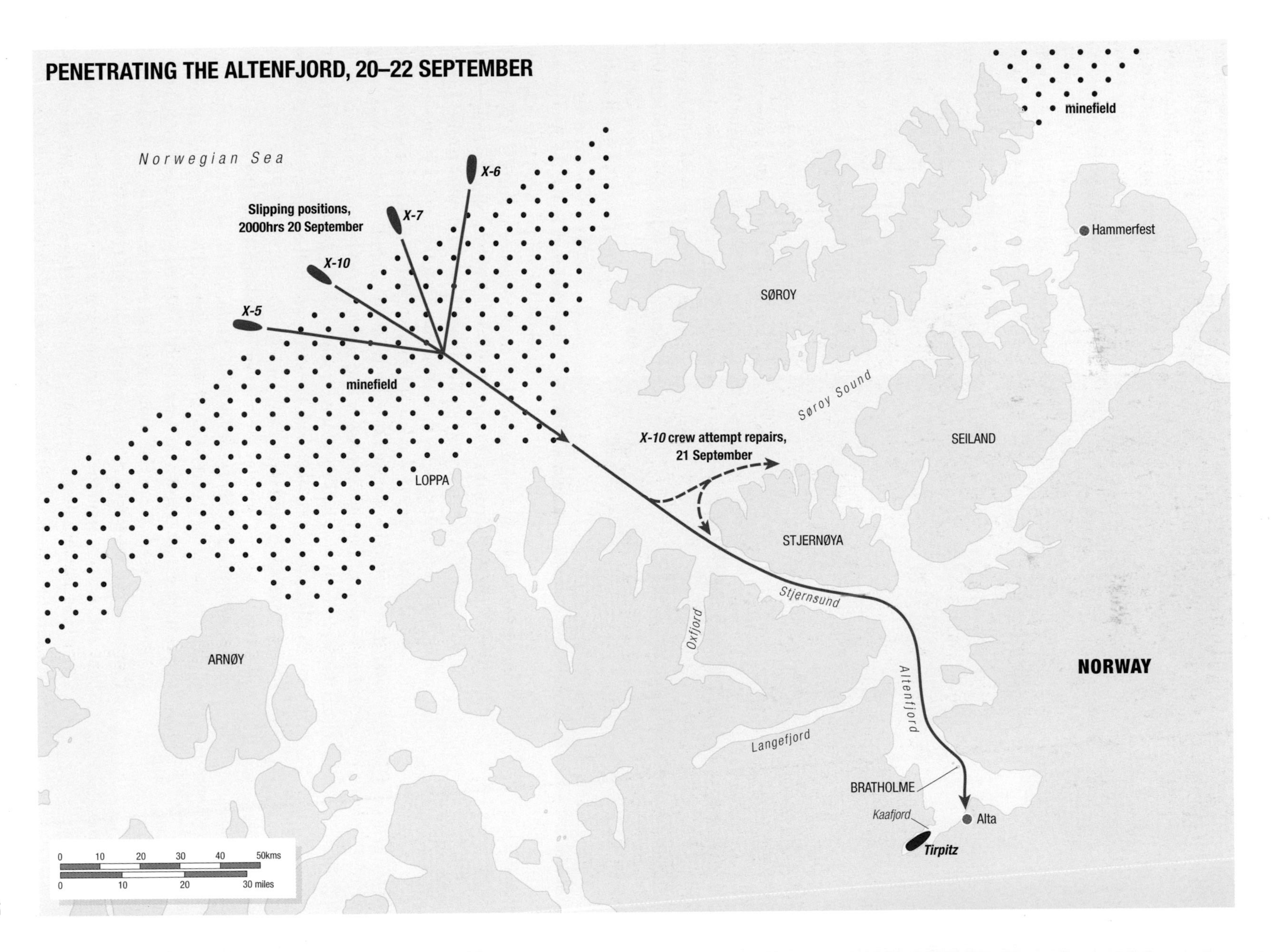
PENETRATING THE ALTENFJORD, 20–22 SEPTEMBER
Norwegian Sea
Slipping positions, 2000hrs 20 September
X-6
X-7
X-10
X-5
minefield
LOPPA
ARNØY
SØROY
Søroy Sound
X-10 crew attempt repairs, 21 September
STJERNØYA
Stjernsund
Oxfjord
Langefjord
Altenfjord
SEILAND
BRATHOLME
Kaafjord
Tirpitz
Alta
Hammerfest
minefield
NORWAY
0 10 20 30 40 50kms
0 10 20 30 miles

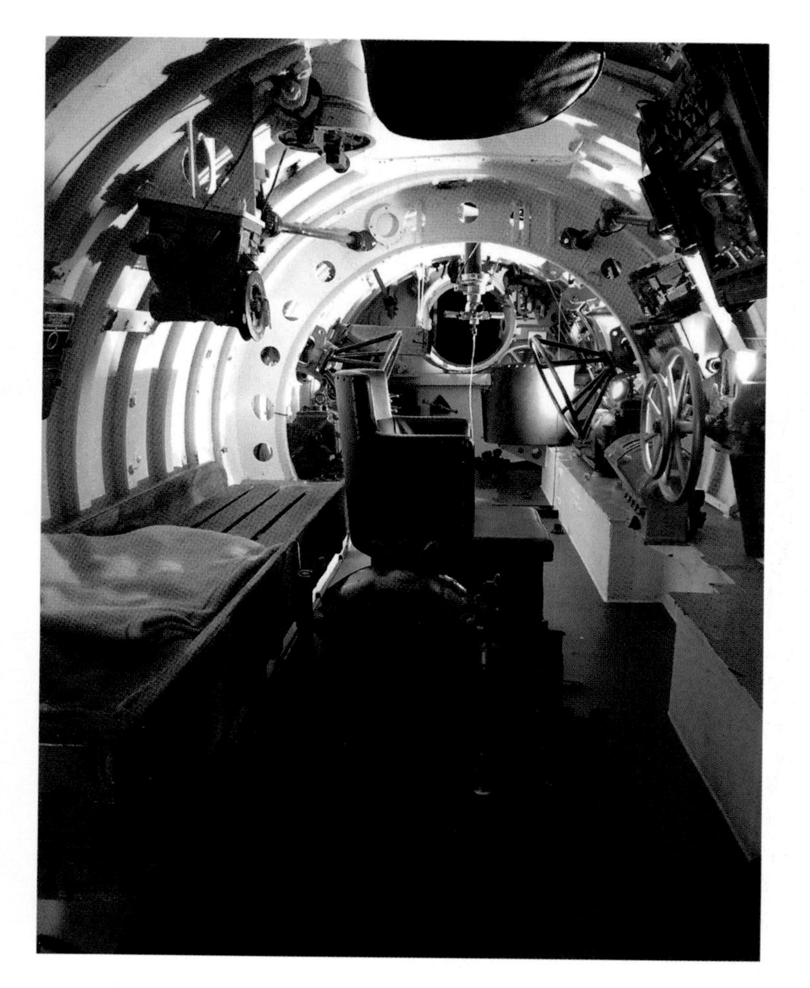

The interior of *X-24*, showing the control room, looking forward towards the hatch leading to the W&D compartment. The chair in the foreground was occupied by the boat's First Lieutenant (second-in-command), while forward of it were the positions of the boat's commander by the periscope, and the engineer. While this looks reasonably spacious, during Operation *Source* this compartment was also filled with stocks of food, supplies, bedding, cooking and sanitation equipment, clothing and escape equipment. (Photograph by Eachan Hardie)

were to be targeted by X-craft, but there was no way to pass on this information to the submariners. They would simply have to find out for themselves. In Scapa Flow, Admiral Fraser, commanding the Home Fleet, called for Operation *Source* to be called off. Meanwhile, he brought his fleet to readiness, in case it had to intercept the German ships somewhere in the Arctic Sea. However, Rear Admiral Barry told him it was impossible to call off the operation, and anyway, *Tirpitz* – its main target – was reportedly still in the Kaafjord. The operation would still go ahead.

The plan called for the X-craft to rendezvous off the north coast of Bratholme Island in the Altenfjord during the late evening of 21 September. An alternative lair was nearby Tømmelholm, a third of a mile away to the north-west. There they could 'guff' and recharge their batteries. The uninhabited island of Bratholme lay 10 miles from the eastern end of the Stjernsund, and according to intelligence reports it was rarely patrolled by the Germans. From there it was just 4½ nautical miles from the mouth of the Kaafjord, and a little over 6 nautical miles to the *Tirpitz* anchorage. *Scharnhorst*'s berth was about 4 nautical miles to the east of the island, while *Lützow* was usually moored half a mile into the Kaafjord, and thus just under 5 nautical miles from the island. Cameron was more than happy to rest his weary crew and recharge the batteries on the surface, particularly as *X-6* had developed a worrying 10-degree list to starboard, which suggested a problem with the starboard ballast tank – exactly what had put *X-8* out of action.

So, at 6.30pm Cameron surfaced off the island. He could see the lights of the small town of Alta 4 miles away to the south, and he knew that the settlement lay at the eastern side of the Kaafjord. The *Tirpitz* was therefore a little further away, down the small fjord. They found a quiet spot to heave to, some 20 yards from the shore, and began recharging their batteries. Cameron had been told that the island was uninhabited, but suddenly a light appeared through the trees. Listening intently, Cameron heard voices. The island was inhabited after all, or at least there was a house there – probably the seasonal dwelling of Norwegian fishermen. He decided that

In this publicity photograph, Sub-Lieutenant Robinson RNVR demonstrates the operation of the main attack periscope of an X-craft. The periscope was powered by a small electric-powered hoisting motor, which turned out to be underpowered and prone to shorting out.

it was unlikely they'd been spotted, so he stayed where he was. While the batteries recharged, the crew of *X-6* settled down to prepare an evening meal of sardines, eggs and cheese, washed down with cocoa.

The food was almost ready to eat when they heard the sound of a diesel engine: a boat was approaching. Then they saw it – a small and sleek-looking patrol boat. Cameron gave the order to shut off the engines, close the hatches and dive where they were. All the time the engine noises were getting closer; as *X-6* slipped under, the boat was less than 40ft away. Through the hull they heard the din of its propellers as she drew closer. They were sure they'd been seen, and expected to hear the sound of depth charges. Instead, the sounds of the propellers gradually faded away. They surfaced again, scraping what remained of their meal off the floor of the control room. For the rest of the night they lay there, undisturbed by German patrols or local fishermen. Inevitably, their thoughts turned to the dangers that lay ahead of them, and to the huge German battleship moored just a few miles away, cocooned in its network of booms and underwater nets.

Meanwhile, Lieutenant Ken Hudspeth of *X-10* was having troubles of his own. *X-10* was due to attack the *Scharnhorst*, which Hudspeth expected to find moored behind the entrance to the Kaafjord at Auskaret, 4½ nautical miles south of Bratholme. However, during his passage through the Søroy minefield the electric motor operating the boat's attack periscope died, leaving the boat partially blind. Then the gyro-compass failed, which made it almost impossible to steer a proper course. Undaunted, the Australian lieutenant pressed on and tried to find a quiet anchorage off the north coast of Søroy where they could try to carry out repairs. At 7am on Tuesday the 21st they put in to the small inlet of Smalfjord and submerged to sit on the bottom, while they set about dismantling both pieces of faulty equipment. They worked on them until the afternoon, eventually getting them working of sorts.

X-10 continued her journey up the Stjernsund, and shortly before midnight they entered the Altenfjord. They were still on the surface, but at about 1.30am they spotted a ship approaching. They dived to 50ft, and the gyro-compass promptly broke down again. They had no idea what course they were steering. Hudspeth came up to periscope depth, hoping to find his bearings. However, the periscope broke down again, amid a smell of burning rubber. *X-10* surfaced to vent the smoke, which at least gave Hudspeth a chance to find out where he was. It was now almost dawn. He saw Tømmelholm and Bratholme a little way off to port, and the entrance to the Kaafjord about 5 miles away off his starboard bow. He steered towards Tømmelholm and submerged off the south-east corner of the island. There they lay on the bottom again until the early hours of Wednesday, 22 September, trying to repair their damaged equipment. It was now just a matter of hours until they were due to carry out their attack on the *Scharnhorst*. Hudspeth realized that without a working periscope and compass his boat had no chance of carrying out her mission. While the other X-craft crept towards their targets, *X-10* remained on the seabed, with her crew becoming increasingly exasperated as the day wore on.

Meanwhile, during the pre-dawn hours of 22 September, the three remaining X-craft – *X-5*, *X-6* and *X-7* – were all making their way towards the Kaafjord. For them there would be no delay, and no turning back. They had encountered difficulties of their own though. *X-6*'s periscope had become flooded, rendering it useless. Still, Cameron was undeterred. He and his crew had come this far: they would now see the thing through.

Lieutenant Place in *X-7* was equally determined, and having recharged his batteries overnight while anchored off the eastern side of Bratholme, he began heading towards the enemy anchorage. He had problems of his own, however. The exhaust pipes of his diesel engine were leaking, filling the boat with fumes. Fortunately, Artificer Bill Whitley saved the day by making a seal out of a strip of canvas, tape and chewing gum. At about 1.30am on Wednesday morning the boat dived, setting a course towards the Kaafjord. As for the remaining boat, *X-5*, for reasons that will shortly be explained its movements during its approach to the Kaafjord are unknown. All we can say for certain is that she reached her objective shortly after dawn that morning, and so was able to play her part in what followed. As for the crew of the *Tirpitz*, they remained blissfully ignorant of the three midget submarines heading towards them.

The approach

The *Tirpitz* lay near the end of the Kaafjord, at the base of a small bay called Barbrudalen. Her stern was moored to the small headland which formed the end of the bay. She was surrounded by two lines of torpedo nets, which formed a box running around the ship, reaching the shore near the end of the headland and halfway up the bay. This was just over 2 miles from

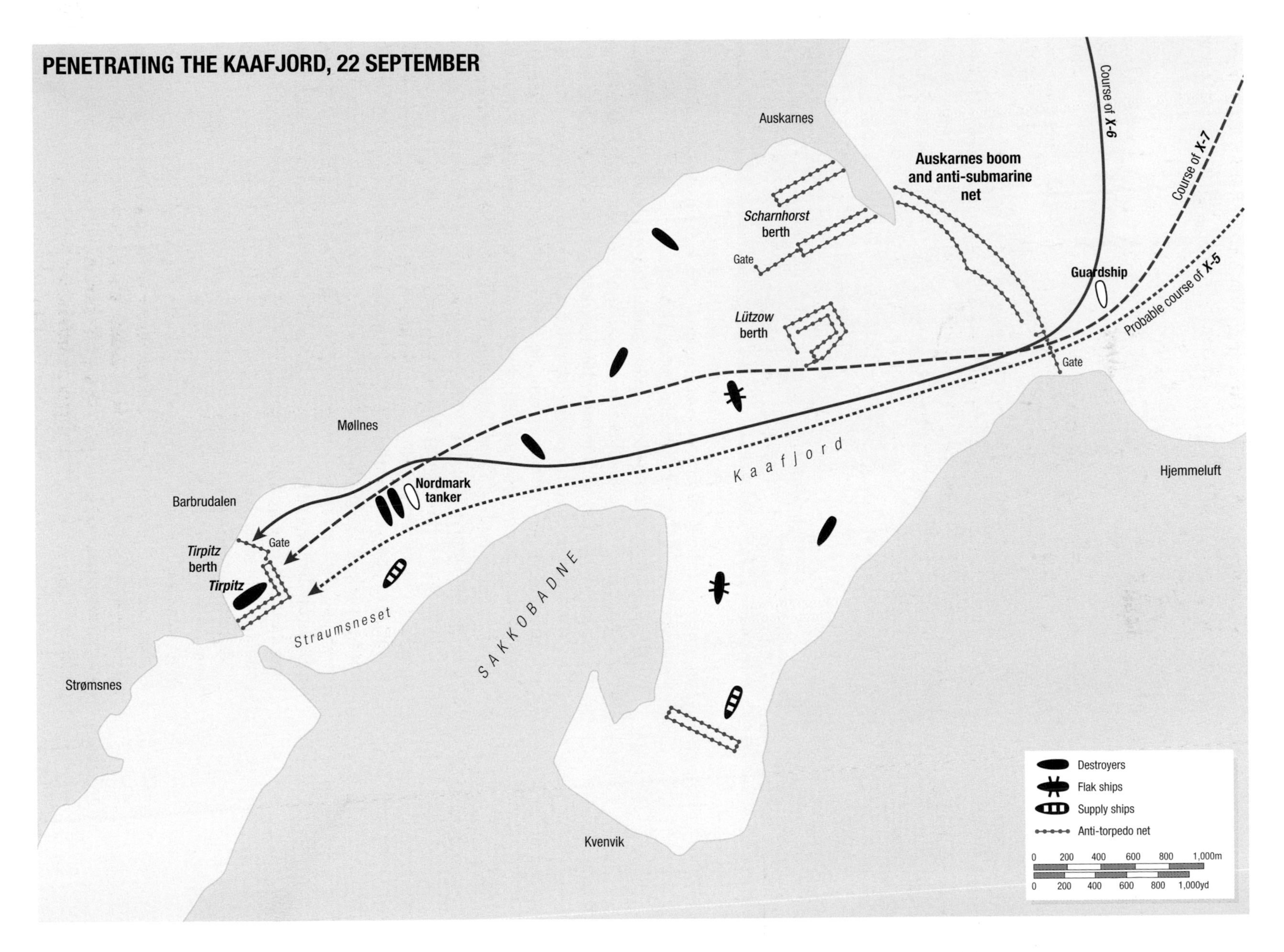
PENETRATING THE KAAFJORD, 22 SEPTEMBER
Auskarnes
Auskarnes boom and anti-submarine net
Course of X-6
Course of X-7
Probable course of X-5
Scharnhorst berth
Gate
Guardship
Lützow berth
Gate
Møllnes
Kaafjord
Hjemmeluft
Nordmark tanker
Barbrudalen
Gate
Tirpitz berth
Tirpitz
Straumsneset
SAKKOBADNE
Strømsnes
Kvenvik
Destroyers
Flak ships
Supply ships
Anti-torpedo net
0 200 400 600 800 1,000m
0 200 400 600 800 1,000yd

The Altenfjord and Kaafjord, based on a photograph taken by a high-flying PRU (Photographic Reconnaissance Unit) aircraft. It shows the mooring of *Tirpitz* behind the headland of Barbrudalen Bay, while beyond it the Auskarnes spit marks the spot where the Kaafjord opens out to the main Altenfjord. The two islands used as a temporary refuge for the X-craft during Operation *Source* can be seen in the top left of the photograph.

the mouth of the Kaafjord, where a narrow spit known as Auskarnes ran southwards for 750 yards into the fjord. This effectively reduced the width of the fjord entrance to just over 1,200 yards. This was blocked by a double line of booms, and the small entrance at its southern end was guarded by a patrol craft, equipped with hydrophones to detect enemy submarines.

Beyond this lay two moorings – one for *Scharnhorst*, tucked up on the western side of the Auskarnes spit, and another a little further into the fjord, where *Lützow* was normally berthed. The attackers didn't know it at the time, but both of these German ships were at sea, so their protected moorings lay empty. Like the *Tirpitz* mooring, these were also protected by double lines of torpedo nets, and were normally guarded by patrol boats. In between them and *Tirpitz* several German warships and support vessels swung at anchor – a small flak ship, a tanker, four destroyers and two supply vessels. *X-5*, *X-6* and *X-7* had to find a way through the Auskarnes boom, and then navigate their way down the fjord to the *Tirpitz* mooring in Barbrudalen Bay. Then they somehow had to penetrate her defensive torpedo nets before working their way beneath the enemy battleship, so they could lay their side charges.

According to the plan, no boat was to attack its target before 1am on 22 September, to allow ample time for all the X-craft to reach their objectives. After that, each X-craft commander had a free hand to make their attack as they saw fit. However, between themselves, Henry Henty-Creer (*X-5*), Donald Cameron (*X-6*) and Godfrey Place (*X-7*) had decided to make their approach to the *Tirpitz* between 5am and 8am, and to set their charges to explode at 8.30am. By then they'd hoped to have left the Kaafjord, and would have reached the relative safety of the Altenfjord.

They had a rough idea of the German defences that lay between them and their objective. The first of these was the Auskarnes boom, which closed off the mouth of the Kaafjord from the tip of the Auskernes spit to Hjemmeluft on the southern side of the fjord. The boom also supported an anti-torpedo net, which had a drop of 157½ft. At the southern end of the channel a 435-yard-long section of the boom could be moved, to allow ships to pass through it. This was guarded by a patrol boat fitted with hydrophones. It had been noted, however, that this moveable gate in the boom was often left open. Once past the boom, the next major obstacle was the Barbrudalen defences, 2 nautical miles to the east, with two layers of anti-torpedo nets, suspended from lines of buoys. The first was just 59ft deep, but the one behind it had a drop of 118ft.

Although this reconnaissance photograph of *Tirpitz* inside her anti-torpedo net enclosure was taken after Operation *Source*, while she was lying in another mooring position, the same arrangement of nets was used. Here you can see them deployed in two lines, just as they were during Operation *Source*.

What intelligence reports hadn't spotted was that there was another 118ft-deep net suspended below the first. In other words, it was a much more formidable obstacle than the three commanders expected. However, there were some gaps in the defences. As at Hjemmeluft, there was a small gate in the net, 66ft wide, at the part that was closest to Barbrudalen. It was there so that the patrol boats guarding the battleship could pass through the defences, along with the ship's own boats. When closed, this was protected by a single anti-torpedo net with a 118ft drop. That night, though, it had been left open, although it was still guarded by a patrol boat equipped with hydrophones. Between Auskernes and Barbrudalen were the destroyers and support ships, all of which might be in a position to detect the midget submarines using hydrophones as they passed by. The task of penetrating these defences was thus a formidable one.

It is not known how *X-5* made her attack, but we can surmise part of it from the evidence. The other two X-craft left their lairs off Bratholme and made their approach to the Kaafjord between 1am and 3am. The sky was overcast and there was a strong north-westerly breeze, which meant that the water of the fjord was covered with small white-capped waves. These were near-perfect conditions for the attackers, as the whitecaps would help hide the wakes of their periscopes. Cameron was particularly grateful for that, as he would have to spend longer on his faulty periscope than normal. He and his crew had also taken the precaution of changing their shoes and socks, in case they had to abandon the submarine and were taken prisoner.

In this copy of a watercolour by submariner Lieutenant Commander John Brooks, a diver is depicted cutting a hole in an anti-submarine net, using his Sarkie Gardner net cutter. This used water and air pressure supplied through a tube connected to the X-craft. During Operation *Source*, none of the boats needed to deploy a diver to penetrate the *Tirpitz's* defences.

Meanwhile, Sub-Lieutenant Dick Kendall struggled into his rubber diving suit, checked his breathing gear and net cutter, then clambered into the W&D compartment. That done, they were fully ready for what lay ahead.

Cameron's biggest problem was his flooded periscope. The boat was fitted with a second search periscope, but this was a stubby thing and could only really be used when the boat was on the surface. He'd need to use the main periscope to locate the boom and anti-torpedo nets at Auskernes, and again at Barbrudalen, and in theory he could use the smaller periscope to guide his way through the nets when submerged, once Kendall had cut a hole in them. It would be a slow, awkward and difficult business, with the ever-present danger of being detected. The approach to Auskernes took longer than they'd expected, and it was nearly 4am when they saw the boom half a mile ahead of them. Unfortunately for them, by then the breeze had died down and the surface of the fjord was still. Then when Cameron raised his periscope again he found it was now completely useless – a green film of water obscured everything. They were completely blind.

Cameron ordered *X-6* to dive to 60ft, then headed towards the southern end of the boom, where the moveable gate was. He also stripped the eyepiece of the periscope and cleaned it. As he approached the net he rose to 30ft, and it was then that he heard the sound of propellers. It was a small boat – probably a patrol boat. He went to periscope depth and raised it. This time the glass remained clear long enough to give him a quick glimpse of the boat. It was a trawler, probably a guardship, and he was just astern of her. The boat was heading directly towards the gate in the nets, which were now open, ready to let her through. Cameron made the split-second decision to follow her. They'd never manage it underwater – the craft was too slow, and the trawler was making about 8 knots – he ordered the engines to go full ahead as soon as the coaming of the boat broke the surface.

The dawn was coming up and the sky was lightening fast, but Cameron reckoned that the low freeboard of the partially submerged X-craft would be hidden by the trawler's wake. However, all it would take would be a sharp-eyed lookout on a patrol boat or a crewman on the trawler looking astern, and they would be spotted. Kendall said later: 'The plan was a little too bold for my taste. I felt it would have been safer to cut through the net than take the risk of revealing our presence.' However, Cameron had made his decision and they were now committed. A few nerve-racking minutes later, and they were through. They'd done it – they were in the Kaafjord. Once there, Cameron took the boat down to 60ft again and headed towards the *Tirpitz*. While they went, they took the periscope apart again, in the hope that they could get it working before they faced their final hurdle.

When running on the surface, only the upper casing of an X-craft such as *X-24* (pictured) was exposed above the water. This made it possible to pull off feats such as *X-6* passing through the anti-submarine defences into the Kaafjord, due to the boat's low silhouette. (Photograph by Eachan Hardie)

While *X-6* had been negotiating the gate into the fjord, Place in *X-7* had already got through the obstacle, having come up with an even more dramatic way of reaching the Kaafjord. They had left Bratholme a little after midnight, and three hours later were in front of the Auskernes boom. Place later wrote that they had hung around for a while off the boom, in order to have enough light to see where they were going. Like Cameron an hour or so later, Place then headed towards the southern portion of the boom and found that the gate at Hjemmeluft was open. He simply stayed submerged and passed through it undetected. This was a huge relief to Sub-Lieutanant Robert Aitken, as his job as the X-craft's diver was to cut a hole in the nets. Aitken later described what happened: 'Just before dawn we set off to the first challenge, the anti-submarine (a/s) net. This was the one the diver had to cut through if the CO [Commanding Officer] couldn't get through it any other way – which all the COs were quite determined to find. As we approached, the CO saw the gate in the a/s net had been opened up to let a trawler through. We dived underneath its wake and got through without having to cut the net.' It was now 3.50am.

Now that *X-7* was in the Kaafjord, Place set a course towards Barbrudalen and the *Tirpitz*. Once there he planned to dive under the double screen of anti-torpedo nets to reach the battleship. However, once through the gate he came up to periscope depth to get his bearings and saw a patrol boat heading close to him. Place gave the order to dive, and the boat passed them by. Again, Aitken recounted the story: 'Having got through the gate the CO, looking through the periscope, saw another boat was about to cross our path. We had to dive below periscope depth, and while unsighted hit a

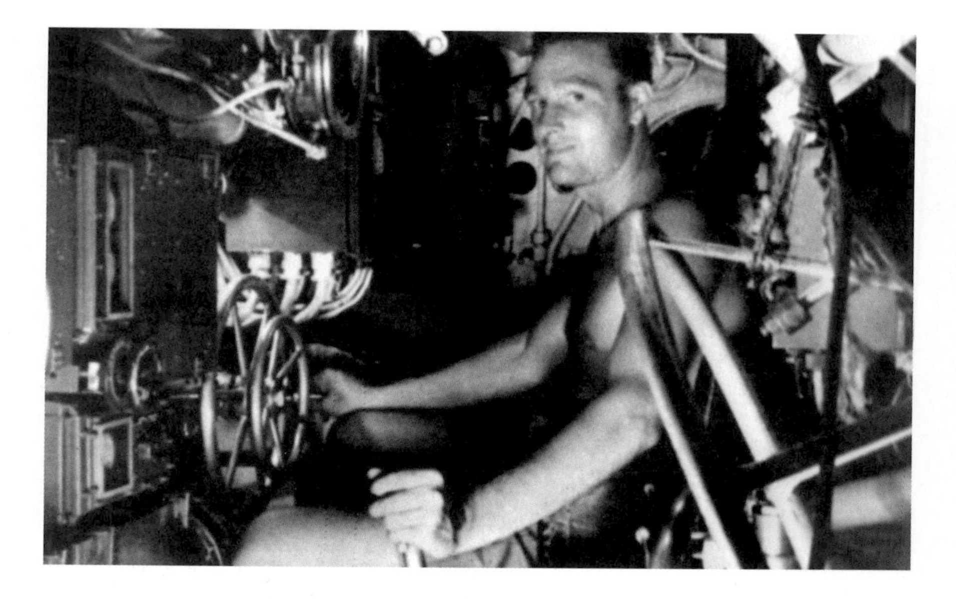

Forward of the periscope was the helm position, occupied by the boat's engineer. As well as steering, the helmsman would control the trim of the boat. Immediately forward of the helmsman's position was the hatch leading to the W&D compartment.

bunch of anti-torpedo (a/t) nets moored in the fjord. In the reconnaissance photograph these nets were protecting a German battleship which had gone to sea.' What had happened was that in the emergency dive and the turn away from the patrol boat, the X-craft veered to starboard, directly into the anti-torpedo nets. Aitken was wrong on one count: these weren't there to protect a battleship. Instead, they'd run into the mooring position of the armoured cruiser *Lützow*.

Place was determined to wriggle free without having to send Aitken into the water. As Place later put it: 'It took quite a while to get out, with quite a lot of pulling and pushing and blowing and so on.' Aitken was more specific: 'All we could do was to shuffle the boat forward and astern, making it alternately more or less buoyant, hoping to shake off the net.' After half an hour they were still stuck, so Place ordered Aitken to get into his rubber diving suit to cut the X-craft free. However, according to Aitken: 'Before I was ready to dive the CO said "Take it off. I don't know how it happened, but we're now free", and we went on our way again.' They continued on towards the *Tirpitz*, which Place reckoned was now a little over 3,000 yards away to the west.

By now though, Place was having problems with his boat. The gyro-compass was developing an intermittent fault, which made it hard to steer a straight course. There was a problem with the trimming pump too, making it difficult to maintain a constant depth when submerged. Still, Place pressed on. He had got within 1½ miles of his target, and he had no intention of aborting the attack. Then at 5.45am, peering through the periscope, Place had his first view of the *Tirpitz*. By then he had successfully worked his way around the moored flak ship the *Thetis* (formerly the Norwegian coastal defence ship *Harald Haarfagre*), a German destroyer and finally the tanker *Noordmark*. Now his target was in sight.

On board *X-6*, Cameron was steering by dead reckoning, heading west towards Barbrudalen. The work on the periscope continued, but it soon became clear that it wasn't going to be much use. All they could see was a dim image through it, and its electric motor had shorted out, which meant they could only raise and lower it by hand. They had a few near misses as they went. First, they passed under the bows of an anchored destroyer, between her and her mooring buoy. If they had been a little closer to the surface they would have struck the destroyer, and their mission would have ended in abject failure. Still, they made it through. *X-6* had another close shave 700 yards further on. This time the obstacle was the tanker *Noordmark*, which was also moored in the fjord. Two German destroyers were tied up alongside her, as if ready to take on fuel. Cameron looked through the periscope and made out the hazy image of the ship and her mooring buoy. This gave him just enough time to alter course hard to starboard and pass around the looming tanker.

As for Henry Henty-Creer and his crew in *X-5*, it is not known how they reached the *Tirpitz*, but according to the Germans no holes were cut in the Auskernes nets, so the probability is that *X-5* had managed to work her way through the boom, as Cameron and *X-6* had done. The X-craft also successfully passed the moored German destroyers and merchant ships, reaching the Barbrudalen anchorage without incident. From what followed, it seems fair to assume she got there a little after *X-6* and *X-7*. Meanwhile, on *Tirpitz*, the unsuspecting crew continued with their normal routine. The crew were roused at 5am, and the hydrophone watch was stood down. Following their normal routine, anti-aircraft watchers were sent ashore and the gate in the anti-torpedo nets was opened to allow small boats to pass to and fro. This would prove a great boon for the attackers, who were now approaching the mighty battleship's lair.

The attack

On board the *X-6*, Cameron struggled to see where he was going. Still, by repeatedly dismantling the eyepiece and cleaning it, he found he was able to see out of a corner of the viewfinder, at least for a short while, until it became obscured again. So, he managed to weave his way through the vessels moored in his path and approach the nets surrounding the *Tirpitz*. Once past these obstructions, they had approached the Barbrudalen moorings by following close to the northern shore of the fjord. That meant the battleship lay off the X-craft's port bow. Between them and their target, of course, was the line of the anti-torpedo nets. He approached them submerged, making 2 knots. He was trying to maintain a depth of 20ft, despite the increasingly erratic trimming pump.

At one point they banged into some obstruction, probably a pontoon built by the Germans on the Barbrudalen shoreline. They also started scraping the bottom of the X-craft on the rocky, fast-sloping shore. Sensibly, Cameron decided to move off towards deeper water, and headed straight across the curve of Barbrudalen Bay. That meant that *X-6* would approach the nets from the north-east. According to his briefing, the nets surrounding *Tirpitz* extended downwards for about 70ft, while the depth of the fjord at that point was about 120ft. By dropping to below the nets, the *X-6* should

▼ EVENTS

1. 7.03am. *X-6* enters the Barbrudalen enclosure through the gate, opened to let a small boat through.
2. 7.07am. *X-6* runs into a submerged rock, and briefly surfaces before her CO, Lieutenant Cameron brings the craft under control and dives again.
3. 7.10am. *X-7* penetrates the anti-torpedo net defences and enters the enclosure.
4. *X-6* accidentally surfaces a second time as Lieutenant Cameron attempts to use his periscope. She is spotted from *Tirpitz*, and the alarm is sounded on the battleship.
5. 7.20am. *X-6* is engaged by small-arms fire from *Tirpitz*, and grenades are thrown at her, until she manages to work her way beneath the battleship's hull. Two minutes later she lays her charges.
6. 7.22am. Having reached *Tirpitz* undetected, Lieutenant Place in *X-7* drops the first of his two charges beneath *Tirpitz*. He then continues down the length of the ship.
7. 7.26am. *X-7* drops her second charge beneath *Tirpitz*, then turns around, heading back towards the anti-torpedo netting.
8. 7.27am. Having been badly damaged, Cameron brings *X-6* to the surface, and the crew scuttle the craft, then abandon her, by boarding a German motor launch. Captain Meyer immediately orders *Tirpitz* to be warped to starboard, using her bow mooring lines, as he suspects the X-craft has laid charges beneath his ship's hull.
9. 7.40am. *X-7* escapes from the enclosure by crossing over the top of the torpedo nets. She is spotted and engaged by small-arms and machine guns.
10. 8.10am. Having dived again then looped round to starboard, *X-7* becomes entangled in the anti-torpedo netting.
11. 8.12am. The charges beneath *Tirpitz* explode, causing extensive damage to the battleship. The shockwaves from these blasts also frees *X-7*.
12. 8.30am. *X-7* surfaces, as her crew attempt to surrender. While Place reaches the safety of a nearby practice target pontoon, the remainder of the crew become trapped in the X-craft as it sinks again.
13. 8.40am. *X-5* surfaces to the south-east of *Tirpitz*, and is fired upon by rifles, machine guns and flak guns. These inflict substantial damage to her, and the boat sinks.
14. 8.41am. Sub-Lieutenant Aitken escapes from the stricken *X-7*, but the remaining two members of her crew are drowned.
15. 8.43am. *X-5* is sunk, and Lieutenant Henty-Creer and his three crew members are lost. For good measure depth charges are then dropped in the vicinity of *X-5* and *X-7*'s last known positions.

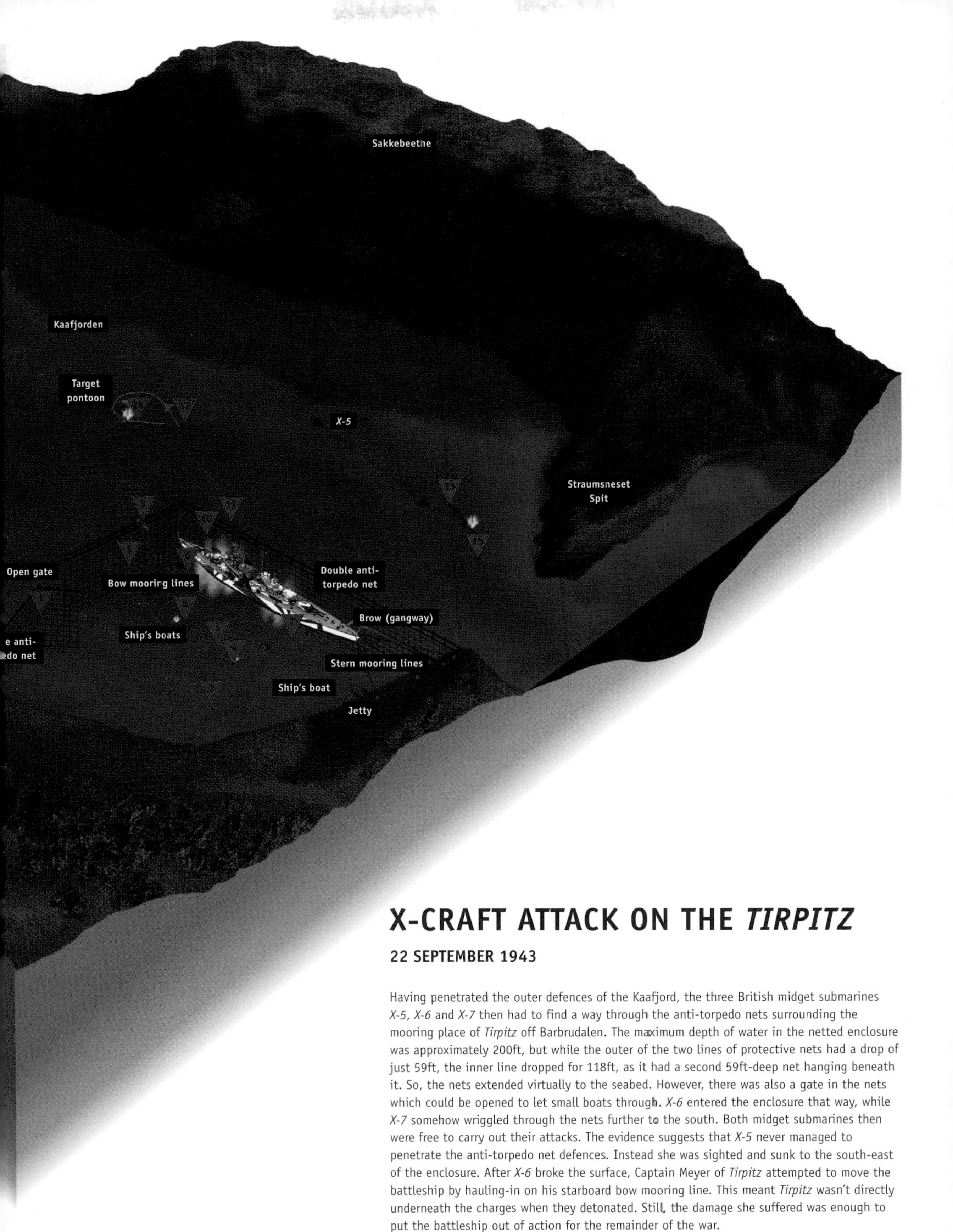

X-CRAFT ATTACK ON THE *TIRPITZ*

22 SEPTEMBER 1943

Having penetrated the outer defences of the Kaafjord, the three British midget submarines *X-5*, *X-6* and *X-7* then had to find a way through the anti-torpedo nets surrounding the mooring place of *Tirpitz* off Barbrudalen. The maximum depth of water in the netted enclosure was approximately 200ft, but while the outer of the two lines of protective nets had a drop of just 59ft, the inner line dropped for 118ft, as it had a second 59ft-deep net hanging beneath it. So, the nets extended virtually to the seabed. However, there was also a gate in the nets which could be opened to let small boats through. *X-6* entered the enclosure that way, while *X-7* somehow wriggled through the nets further to the south. Both midget submarines then were free to carry out their attacks. The evidence suggests that *X-5* never managed to penetrate the anti-torpedo net defences. Instead she was sighted and sunk to the south-east of the enclosure. After *X-6* broke the surface, Captain Meyer of *Tirpitz* attempted to move the battleship by hauling-in on his starboard bow mooring line. This meant *Tirpitz* wasn't directly underneath the charges when they detonated. Still, the damage she suffered was enough to put the battleship out of action for the remainder of the war.

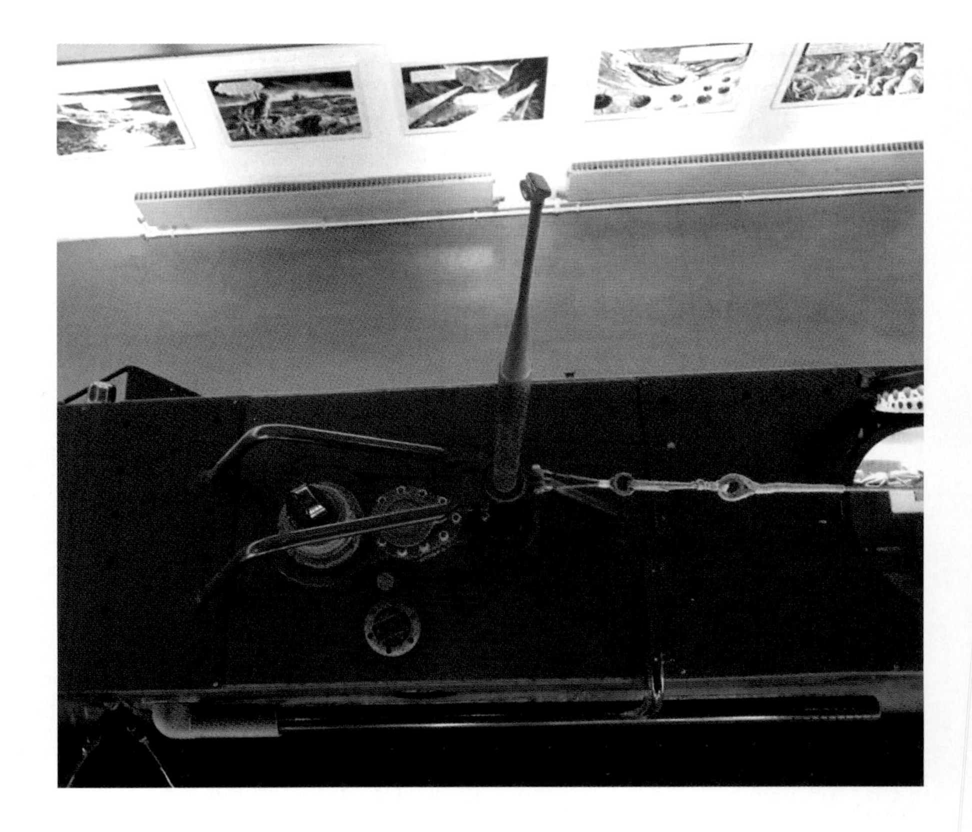

The attack periscope of *X-24*, fully extended. Forward of it is the smaller stubby night periscope, protected by a pair of rails. A small observation scuttle lies between the two. Astern of the periscope is the open aft hatch, which led directly into the boat's control room. (Photograph by Eachan Hardie)

thus be able to penetrate the anti-torpedo defences with comparative ease. Raising the periscope for a final look around, Cameron gave the order to dive to 60ft. He would have to drop under the net defence, then make his way to the battleship based on dead reckoning.

To Cameron, the battleship looked majestic as it lay moored there, less than 300 yards in front of him. As he turned the periscope from the battleship to the line of net buoys, peering through that little sliver of vision he had, the periscope motor short-circuited with a loud bang and a flash. Smoke filled the control room as a small electrical fire started, but it was soon put out. Still, Cameron had seen what he needed. Once through the obstacle of the nets he would surface inside the mooring area, take a final bearing of *Tirpitz* and then head towards her to lay his side charges.

By now, however, *X-6* was in a bad way. The ballast tank on the port side had flooded, so the boat was listing heavily. So far they had managed to compensate for that, but the list was increasing, and soon Cameron would have to jettison the whole side charge. Still, they struggled on as he was determined to do this as close as he possibly could to the target. The tank was also sending up a stream of air bubbles, which made detection by the defenders far more likely. It now looked as if they wouldn't make it out of the fjord after the attack. For now though, their minds were focussed on the task in hand – penetrating the defences and laying their charges. Their mood was summed up by Sub-Lieutenant John Lorimer. Just as they were diving to get under the nets, he said to Cameron: 'Let's see what she's worth, Skipper.' Whatever the problems, they would press on.

Having dived to 60ft, Cameron tried to pass under the nets, but ran straight into them. They backed up a little and dived another 20ft: the same thing happened. Cameron ordered them to reverse engines a little and drop down to 100ft. Once more they ran into the net, which clearly dropped much further than intelligence reports had suggested. Cameron reckoned they went all the way to the seabed. Reluctant to send Sub-Lieutenant Kendall out of the X-craft to cut their way through the nets, Cameron came up to periscope depth again. It was then that he spotted the open boat gate in the nets, just a few yards away on his starboard beam. Spotting a German picket boat – a large ship's launch – making its way through the gate and heading for the battleship, he decided to repeat his trick at Auskernes and follow the vessel through.

With the picket boat almost right above them, Cameron turned onto the same heading. He was now riding underneath her at periscope depth: they could actually feel their periscope bumping and scraping against the underside of the boat before it forged ahead of them, leaving them in its wake. Then they were through. Looking through his periscope, when Cameron saw they were clear he gave the order to dive. Amazingly, it looked like they hadn't been detected. They were inside the nets, and the *Tirpitz* would be lying ahead and to the left of them, a little over 100 yards away. Cameron spun the periscope round and saw that behind him, the Germans were closing the gate again. He told the crew. As Edmund Goddard, the boat's Engine Room Artificer, put it; 'Well, we've had it then, as far as changing our minds!' It was now 7.05am.

By Cameron's reckoning they had little enough time to set their charges, drop them beneath the battleship and make their way out of the netted enclosure. It would take even longer to make it all the way to Auskernes, passing through the nets there too. The trouble was, he had planned to make his attack at 6.30am. The charges were due to be detonated at 8.30am, which would have given them two hours to make their escape. Now that was reduced to just 90 minutes. While he could time his own charges to suit the situation, he had no idea whether *X-5* and *X-7* had penetrated the inner defences. If they had, then their charges would almost certainly go off at the prearranged time. He therefore had to get on with the task, and *X-6* had to somehow make its way out of the Barbrudalen enclosure, putting as much distance between itself and the battleship as it could.

After taking a last look at the battleship through his now almost completely useless periscope, Cameron gave the order to dive to get beneath the *Tirpitz*. All this time they had been slipping through the water at a little under 2 knots. By his calculations, if they continued on their present course they would run aground on the eastern side of the headland which formed the end of Barbrudalen Bay. He decided to alter course to port and swing round towards the stern of the battleship. It was at this point that they rammed into a submerged rock. The impact was enough to throw Cameron against the gyro-compass, and Kendall had to grab on to stop himself being thrown to the deck. The noise of the impact had been loud, and Cameron was sure someone on the battleship would have heard it. However, worse

The passage and operational crews of *X-6*. Back (left to right): Lieutenant Wilson, Lieutenant Cameron, Sub-Lieutenant Lorimer. Front (left to right): Sub-Lieutenant Kendall, ER Artificer Goddard, Stoker Oakley, Leading Seaman McGregor.

was to follow. After striking the rock, the bows of *X-6* were forced upwards at an angle of almost 60 degrees. The boat was surging upwards towards the surface of the fjord.

The midget submarine broke the surface some 200 yards from the German battleship's port quarter, but Cameron managed to get the boat under control and it slipped back under the surface. On board the *Tirpitz*, a petty officer was standing next to his flak gun when he spotted something in the water. He called out to a duty chief petty officer, and told him he'd just seen a submarine. This claim was met with scepticism, largely because no submarine could have operated in such shallow water. He suggested it might be a porpoise, or even a dolphin. Part of the problem was that the ship's second-in-command, Captain Heinz Assmann, had carried out no end of drills over the past few months, testing the battleship's defences. There had been so many exercises, and then false alarms by jumpy lookouts, that the crew were quite jaded. So, rather than facing being mocked by their shipmates for sounding a false alarm, the two NCOs said nothing about the mysterious sighting.

Tirpitz had a hydrophone watch, and if they had been operating, these underwater sound-detectors might well have heard *X-6* colliding with the rock. However, they had been switched off that morning, as they were due to be overhauled later that day, so nobody heard the crash. It was now 7.07am, and *X-6*, still undetected, was creeping towards the battleship's port side. Unfortunately for Cameron, the collision had finally put the gyro-compass out of action, so he had no real idea where he was heading. He had to work by dead reckoning. Still, he worked out that in about two minutes, if they held their current depth of 70ft, they would eventually run into the lower hull of the battleship, somewhere amidships. However, after three minutes nothing had happened. The miniature submarine was badly wallowing now, having been damaged in the collision. Cameron decided to take her up to periscope depth, but the trim was upset, and instead of stopping at 15ft, the craft surged on upwards and again broke the surface of the fjord.

All of the Operation *Source* passage and operational crews for the six X-craft, gathered on the deck of HMS *Bonaventure*. Of the 42 British and Commonwealth submariners who served in these boats, nine would lose their lives during the operation.

Cameron could see they were now about 75 yards off the port beam of the battleship, close to a pair of picket boats which were secured to her side. This time he surfaced in plain view of several German sailors, and the alarm was raised. It was 7.12am. The alarm that was sounded though, was a misleading one. On the bridge the officer-of-the-day ordered the sounding of five short blasts on the ship's horn. This called for men to close watertight doors, not to man their guns and shoot at a submarine. Precious moments were wasted as the crew tried to figure out what was happening. That gave Cameron time to dive again and edge closer to the battleship. He had originally planned to lay his charges under the battleship's stern, as that would render *Tirpitz* immobile, even if she stayed afloat. However, he now had to be content with laying them somewhere near the battleship's bow. That is, of course, if he and his men weren't blown out of the water first.

The idea was to head towards the *Tirpitz* and peer through the periscope while submerged. When he spotted a shadow, he reckoned he would be approaching the battleship, and would put the engines in reverse to take the momentum off the craft. He would then dive, lay his side charges and try to escape through the nets by the way he had come in. Without any warning, the boat then ran into something and came to a halt. It turned out to be wires hanging off the battleship's port side, near the bow, which effectively entangled the X-craft. Lorimer tried to break free by powering the craft forward and back, but then, when it did come loose, *X-6* shot to the surface again some 20 yards from the battleship's bows. German crewmen were lining the deck, firing rifles at them and lobbing grenades into the water. The *X-6* crew could all now see the *Tirpitz* through the small viewing ports. She looked immense, the dark hull towering above them and stretching aft as far as they could see.

The side charge of an X-craft weighed 4 tons, and was held in place to the flank of the boat by means of a thick pin. It could be released from inside the submarine, after the boat's commander set the clock time fuse. The charge itself consisted of 2 tons of the military-grade chemical explosive Amatex.

Now they were detected, it was unlikely they'd make it out of the Barbrudalen enclosure, let alone the Kaafjord. As grenades started detonating around them, the concussion reverberated through the small boat like giant hammers. As Cameron noted afterwards, the only good thing about the situation was that they were now too close to the battleship for her guns to bear on them. He took the only sensible course available to him, giving the order to dive. As they sank towards the bed of the fjord, Lorimer gently powered the boat forward, creeping towards the underside of the target's hull. At 7.22am, Cameron detached the two side charges, which dropped towards the seabed, almost directly under the battleship's foredeck, level with 'Bertha' turret. He set the charges to go off in an hour – roughly the time that had been arranged back on board the *Bonaventure* in Loch Cairnbawn. In theory, they had completed their mission.

Now came the problem of survival. The chances of making it out of the enclosure were now non-existent. The only way out was to surface, scuttle *X-6* and give themselves up. First, though, they had to destroy everything they could that the Germans might find useful, such as charts, orders, schedules and signal books. They burned what they could, which simply made the fetid atmosphere in the small craft even worse. Then Cameron gave the order to surface. When they did, the crew would open the sea cocks, putting the electric motor telegraph astern with the hydroplanes set for diving. That way the X-craft would sink rapidly, ideally leaving them just enough time to scramble out. They might be shot, but it was really the only chance they had.

In the end they were lucky. When *X-6* broke the surface for the third time that morning, they appeared just a few yards from a German motor launch. The battleship's crew were still firing at them, but the four British submariners scrambled out of the hatch, led by Goddard, who held his hands up. He was followed by Kendall, who did the same, then Lorimer and finally Cameron. Clearly surrendering, the firing slackened as the German launch came alongside. Covered by German sailors with rifles, the four crew stepped off their sinking X-craft and into the launch. As Kendall said later: 'We didn't even get our feet wet.' Meanwhile, the crew of the motor launch tried to take the X-craft in tow, but when she began to sink they were forced to cut the line or risk being towed under with her. So, unlike her crew, *X-6* avoided being captured.

Cameron and his three companions were taken on board the *Tirpitz*, keenly aware that in less than an hour 4 tons of Amatex high explosives would detonate directly beneath them. The launch reached the battleship's port gangway, and the four prisoners clambered up it to the quarterdeck. John Lorimer was in the lead, and he paused when he reached the battleship's vast quarterdeck, where more sailors were covering them with rifles. He turned to Cameron and asked: 'Skipper ... shall we salute the German flag?' Grinning, Cameron answered: 'Why, of course!' They both duly 'chopped off' as neat a salute as they could manage, to the bewilderment of their German captors. They were then searched, and stripped of their possessions, such as watches, wallets, photographs and even Cameron's pipe. As they did, they glanced at their confiscated watches. The time was now 7.36am; their charges were due to go off in just 44 minutes.

Although Cameron, Lorimer, Kendall and Goddard didn't know it, the other two X-craft had also broken in to the Kaafjord and were carrying out their own attacks. At roughly 7am, just a few minutes behind *X-6*, Godfrey Place in *X-7* had reached the Barbrudalen nets. Just like Cameron, Place had been told there were two lines of anti-torpedo nets protecting the battleship, but that these probably didn't extend any deeper that 70ft, which should give him some 50ft of clearance to slip under them. He approached them at about 80ft – or as close to that as his damaged trim tanks allowed – and *X-7* promptly ran into them. They managed to wriggle the boat free after five minutes of manoeuvring. This had been disorienting, so Place decided to come to the surface to see where they were. As he put it later: 'Miraculously, when we came up to the surface there were no intervening nets, and the *Tirpitz* was 50 to 60ft away.'

_X-7_ penetrating _Tirpitz_'s net defences, 22 September 1943 (overleaf)

Just after 7am on 22 September, *X-7*, travelling at periscope depth, approached the anti-torpedo net defences protecting *Tirpitz*'s moorings at Barbrudalen in the Kaafjord. The commander of *X-7*, Lieutenant Godfrey Place, thought it unlikely that the nets extended for more than 70ft from the surface. However, despite diving to 80ft, just 40ft from the seabed, they still found nets in front of them. There were actually two layers of nets, and one of them extended to the seabed. At that point Place was reluctant to send his diver, Sub-Lieutenant Robert Aitken, out to cut a hole in them. Instead, he tried manoeuvring the boat in an attempt to wriggle his way through the obstruction. What followed was later described by Place as 'blowing and wriggling', as he tried everything he could to find a way through the nets. After several minutes, the X-craft broke free of the obstruction. The likelihood is that *X-7* managed to duck under the first net line, then wriggle through a gap between the upper and lower nets of the second, more substantial barrier, a few yards behind the first. Here, we see *X-7* as she looked when she first began probing the nets, and Place realized that the defences were far more formidable than he had imagined.

Small-arms fire, machine guns and light flak guns open up on the midget submarine *X-7*, when she surfaced off the starboard bow of *Tirpitz* during the closing stages of the attack. Behind the boat is the towed target raft which Lieutenant Place managed to reach after his boat sank beneath him.

Later, Aitken tried to explain the 'miracle': 'The CO tried to find a way through the a/t nets protecting the *Tirpitz*. He tried one way after another, and I don't think Godfrey Place was ever absolutely sure how, but he suddenly found we were inside the nets surrounding the *Tirpitz*. Without knowing it, the CO may have slid over the top, found a gap, or the open gate.' However they managed it, *X-7* was now inside the enclosure, only a short distance from their target. The time was 7.10am. The midget submarine was close to its target, and Place could see it through his periscope, but the gyro-compass wasn't working: to approach the *Tirpitz* when fully submerged, he would have to use dead reckoning. He dived the boat to 40ft, then moved forward at 2 knots. At 7.22am they banged into the underside of the battleship, somewhere below 'Bruno' turret. This, strangely, was exactly where Cameron was headed moments earlier.

Place duly released his first charge beneath 'Bruno'. After slamming into the *Tirpitz*, the *X-7* was deflected to starboard and began travelling down the length of the battleship's hull, heading towards the stern. He still had his second charge, which he released further down the battleship's hull, just forward of 'Caesar' turret. Place then turned the X-craft to starboard and cruised back down the side of the battleship, until he passed clear of her bows. They had done it. Their charges were laid, timed to go off in a little over an hour. Now they had to find a way out of the enclosure and reach the open waters of the Kaafjord.

Afterwards, Place recalled how hard it was to escape from the enclosure: 'In that area it was very difficult to pinpoint yourself precisely. So, in fact we spent most of the next three quarters of an hour trying to find the way out. I think we passed under the ship two or three times. Our charges were set for an hour, and by then it occurred to me that we needed to take somewhat drastic measures to get out.' This is exactly what he did. Having figured out where the double line of nets were, he tried what he later described as 'a new technique for getting out of nets'. He surfaced, switched to diesel power and set the engines to full ahead. As a result, as he put it: 'We did a sort of flop operation of hitting the net, holding ourselves down, blowing the bow tanks to full buoyancy as fast as we could, so we came up with a terrific angle, and at the same time going full ahead on the motor, scraping the top of the net and got out.' The time was now about 7.40am.

The *Tirpitz*, manoeuvring in the Altenfjord with the assistance of tugs. On 22 September 1943, the battleship's commander Captain Meyer realized that he was facing a threat from underwater explosive charges, but was unable to move *Tirpitz* out of the way. The best he could do was to move her slightly using his bow mooring lines, so the charges didn't detonate directly beneath his ship's hull.

As soon as *X-7* surfaced and scraped over the nets, the Germans realized there was another submarine there. Almost immediately, rifle and machine-gun bullets swept the boat's casing. Place dived *X-7* and veered off to starboard. He didn't have time to look back at *Tirpitz*, because, as he put it later, his attempt to cross the nets was 'new and absorbing'. On board the *Tirpitz*, the four British submariners held under guard on the quarterdeck saw *X-7* break the surface and noticed something the Germans weren't aware of. They saw that she wasn't carrying her side charges. That meant that rather than 4 tons of high explosives beneath them, in all probability there was twice that, set to explode in less than an hour's time.

After crossing the nets, *X-7* dived to 60ft and travelled another 200 yards. By then there were problems with the boat – both steering and maintaining trim had become difficult, although the craft was still structurally sound. As a result they circled round and ran into another net – the outer anti-torpedo net at the south-east corner of the Barbrudalen enclosure. As Place said later: 'We tried to come to the surface or to periscope depth for a look, so that the direction indicator could be started, and as much distance as possible put between ourselves and the coming explosion. It was extremely annoying therefore, to run into another net at 60ft.' The time was now about 8.10am, and the crew of *X-7* realized they would have little or no chance to get out of the area before their charges went off.

These charges, together with the ones laid by *X-6*, were timed to go off at 8.30am – in about 20 minutes' time – if the charge timers worked perfectly. Meanwhile, having realized that his ship was being attacked by midget submarines, Captain Hans Meyer, commanding the *Tirpitz*, ordered the general alarm to be sounded. This might well have saved his ship. The battleship's crew rushed to their action stations, and all watertight doors were closed. By then, Meyer realized that the submarines weren't using torpedoes: that meant some kind of underwater charge, either attached to the underside of his hull or else dropped on the seabed underneath the ship. While German divers suited up to inspect the hull, the engine room staff also began raising steam. That would take an hour, and without tugs, moving the battleship would be tricky within the net enclosure.

As a precaution, Meyer ordered the duty watch of seamen to begin moving the ship to starboard, by veering or loosening the port-side mooring at the bow and hauling in on the starboard one. There were too many mooring lines at the stern to move the whole ship in a hurry. As a result, the bows of the battleship slowly began turning to starboard. Meyer's idea was that if any charges had been deposited on the seabed beneath the ship, then he would move the battleship just enough so that they would explode off his port side, rather than directly under the hull. His intention was ultimately to move out of the anchorage and take up position on the far side of the fjord. By now he had realized that the biggest threat to his ship lay with ground mines laid by these midget submarines, rather than from smaller limpet mines attached to the hull. He and his men did what they could, but it was a matter of too little, too late.

With the ship clearly under attack, Captain Meyer ordered that the two senior prisoners, Cameron and Lorimer, be taken below to cabins at 8am for questioning. They only gave their interrogators the most basic information, all the while keenly aware of the clock ticking down on the charges beneath their feet. Lorimer said later that he felt he could hardly breathe with the anticipation, and could feel his heart racing. "At 8.12am the charges went off with an almighty explosion; it felt as if the battleship was lifted several feet into the air." The charges had gone off prematurely. There were actually two near-simultaneous explosions. The first came from the bow, beneath 'Bruno' turret, where the three charges there went off simultaneously. This was followed a second or two later by the fourth charge further aft, beneath 'Caesar' turret.

Lorimer was thrown off his chair and onto the deck, and he recalled that the whole ship oscillated like a steel whip for several seconds. Dozens of the crew working on the upper deck were hurled into the air, and one was killed as he landed head-first on an anchor cable. Others were injured, mainly with limbs broken or skulls fractured. The ship began listing to port, a large hole having been blown in her port side, near the bows. Everywhere below decks there was smoke from short-circuits, along with broken glass, while steam gushed from severed pipes. Doors were jammed either shut or open, and hatches slammed shut. Foam was spraying out of fire-fighting equipment, adding to the confusion. Cameron and Lorimer could hear the sound of water flooding into the ship. They were plunged into darkness too, until the emergency power was restored. The neat and orderly battleship had been plunged into chaos.

Cameron and Lorimer were marched back to their companions on the quarterdeck. There, as Lorimer put it: 'Sailors were rushing about, there was a lot of fist shaking at us, and all the small guns seemed to be firing.' Presumably, after the surfacing of *X-7*, they were shooting at whatever looked like a midget submarine. The submariners were marched over and lined up against a bulkhead, guarded by a line of sailors with machine pistols. An officer appeared with a pistol in his hand and kept shouting 'How many?' at them – presumably referring either to the number of midget submarines or the charges they'd laid. All four of the submariners were convinced they were about to be shot. Then, a senior officer came up the stern gangway and approached them. It was Admiral Oskar Kummetz, the Kriegsmarine's fleet commander in Norwegian waters. He ordered the officer to treat his captives as prisoners of war, and so, thanks to the admiral, they were spared a summary execution.

Grossadmiral Erich Raeder (front), head of the Kriegsmarine, pictured during an inspection tour of the *Tirpitz*. Following him is Generaladmiral Otto Schniewind, commander of the Kriegsmarine's Gruppe Nord (Group North). On the far right is Vizeadmiral Oskar Kummetz, the fleet commander of the naval battle group in Norway. It was Kummetz who spared the lives of the surviving crew members of *X-6* and *X-7*.

Meanwhile, in the *X-7*, Place and his companions were little more than 150 yards away from the charges when they went off. They were thrown about in the boat. As Place put it: 'A quite considerable amount of noise, really rather too close to us for any comfort, but by no means lethal. The aft hatch lifted, and quite a volume of water came in, and there were one or two small spurting leaks, but nothing too dramatic.' The damage was actually quite severe – it just took the submariners time to realize. The jolt, though, had freed the X-craft from the nets, so Place took the boat to periscope depth to have a look. He was disheartened to see that the *Tirpitz* was still there, and there seemed little sign of damage. They returned to the bottom of the fjord to decide what to do next.

Navigation was a problem, as neither the gyro-compass nor the periscope were working. Most of their dials and gauges had been shattered, the

Lieutenants Godfrey Place RN (left) and Donald Cameron RNR were held as prisoners of war after their capture in the Kaafjord. Both men were awarded the Victoria Cross for their exploits during Operation *Source*. This picture was taken shortly after their release.

trimming tanks were damaged, and although the X-craft still seemed structurally sound, she was leaking badly. They soon found they were unable to maintain a steady depth, as the water inside the boat kept moving from one end of the craft to the other as soon as they tried to surface or descend. It became clear that *X-7* was inoperable. The decision was made to surface, then to try to abandon the boat. The danger was that they would be cut down by enemy fire as they clambered out. It was decided that Place would lead the way, waving a white flag – or rather a grubby white submariner's jersey.

They brought the boat up, and Place clambered out of the W&D hatch, with Aitken following behind. The Germans immediately opened up with machine-gun and rifle fire, and before Aitken could make it onto the coaming the craft gave a lurch and water began flooding in through the hatch. He slammed it shut and the boat started sinking. Place found they were right next to a wooden platform – a floating target used by the battleship's gunnery. He leaped onto it as *X-7* went under. The time was now 8.35am. He kept waving the white jumper, and soon a German boat appeared and took him aboard. He was taken to the *Tirpitz*, where he joined the other prisoners. On board *X-7*, Robert Aitken, Bill Whittam and Bill Whitley were still trapped inside the craft when she sank, with more water flooding into the boat. The batteries began leaking fumes, so they donned their breathing sets and waited until the boat was fully flooded so they could open the hatch and escape.

The wait was too long for Whitley. After struggling with the hatch, Aitken turned to see his body floating in the control room, having run out of oxygen. Then the hatch opened and Aitken shoved himself through it. When he broke the surface he looked around for Whittam, but could not see him. He saw *Tirpitz* though, and remembered thinking that it was a great disappointment to see her afloat. Aitken was soon rescued by a German boat, and within minutes he had joined the other prisoners on board the *Tirpitz*. Whittam and Whitley went down with their boat. Of the eight men who crewed *X-6* and *X-7*, two had died during the final moments of the operation, while the other six had been taken prisoner.

One of the mysteries of the operation was the fate of *X-5*. At 8.43am, lookouts on *Tirpitz* spotted a third midget submarine break the surface of the fjord, roughly 500 yards off the battleship's starboard bow. She was therefore well outside the anti-torpedo nets. This was *X-5*, commanded by Lieutenant Henry Henty-Creer. She was targeted by German small-arms and automatic weapons, including flak guns. She was seen to sink, but for good measure a destroyer dropped several depth charges in the area. The X-craft and her crew never reappeared. Uncertainty has shrouded *X-5*'s part in the operation ever since, until in 2003, Norwegian divers found the wreck of a midget submarine in the Kaafjord. Some 300 yards from it was an unexploded side charge, which presumably had been detached from *X-5* during the operation.

So, it appeared that Henty-Creer and his crew did attempt to attack the *Tirpitz*, but presumably they had suffered damage, were forced to surface and were duly sunk by enemy fire and depth charges. The Australian-born Henty-Creer, together with his crew – Sub-Lieutenant Alastair Malcolm, Sub-Lieutenant Tom Nelson and Engine Room Artificer Ralph Mortiboys – all perished. Claims they had managed to exit the Kaafjord, and even reach the Altafjord the following day were never proven. Officially they were missing in action, and so never completed their mission. While Cameron and Place were both awarded the Victoria Cross, and their crews were also decorated, the gallantry of the four men in *X-5* was never officially recognized. Some have seen this as an injustice. However, until the remains of the X-craft in the fjord are fully examined, the full part they played in the drama may never be known.

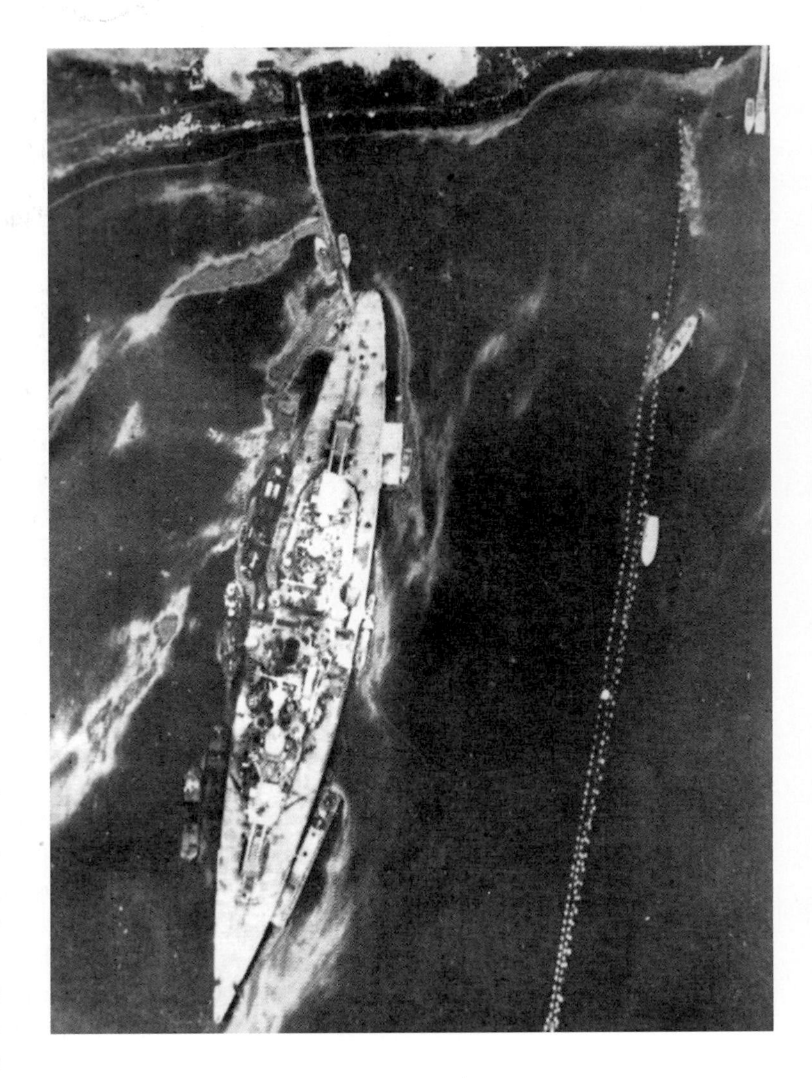

The *Tirpitz* after the attack, in a photograph taken by a PRU reconnaissance flight. The battleship is riding low in the water at the bow, and an extensive oil leak can be seen around her. A pontoon has been placed against the port side of her forecastle, allowing emergency repair work to be carried out on the damage caused by the three underwater explosive charges that detonated below 'Bruno' turret.

By 9am, the X-craft raid on the *Tirpitz* was over. She had survived the detonation of some 8 tons of high explosives under her keel, and to the disappointed British submariners who survived, looked to still be fully operational. However, the damage suffered by the German battleship soon turned out to be far more extensive than had first been thought. This would only become apparent in the days and weeks following 22 September. The whole operation had cost the lives of nine British submariners, and the loss of all but one of the X-craft. It was a high cost for what seemed at first to be such a negligible result. However, as the full facts began to emerge, the British Admiralty were finally able to conclude that the raid – Operation *Source* – had been a resounding success.

AFTERMATH

The straggler

Of the six X-craft which took part in the raid, by the mid-morning of Wednesday, 22 September only one of them was left. Lieutenant Ken Hudspeth and his crew in *X-10* had spent the night on the seabed off Tømmelholm, some 4½ miles from the *Tirpitz*. The whole crew wanted to continue with their attack on the *Scharnhorst*, but they realized their submarine had no chance of success unless it could be repaired. So they remained where they were. As the diver, Sub-Lieutenant Geoff Harding, put it: 'We would stay on the bottom to hear if any of the bangs occurred at the appointed times. If they didn't, we would go in and have a bash ourselves. It was reassuring to know that while we were near enough to the *Tirpitz* and *Scharnhorst* to hear the bangs, we were far enough away to be out of range of the big blast that we hoped that morning would bring.'

They expected 'the bangs' at 8.30am, and while they continued to work at trying to repair their boat and its equipment, they kept an ear cocked for the sound of explosions. Harding summed up the mood in the boat: 'We felt like kids at a Punch and Judy show, knowing that Punch was about to hit Judy, and enjoying the fact that Judy didn't know. The bangs came ... and were a lovely sound... We stayed on the bottom all that day, and I think we were all feeling very mixed inside. We were glad about the bangs, but sad that they weren't ours.' Finally, at 6pm, Hudspeth had no option but to admit defeat. It was clear that any attempt to attack *Scharnhorst* without a working periscope or gyro-compass was doomed to failure, so he called off the attack. As Rear Admiral Barry reported of Hudspeth's decision: 'He showed good judgement in coming to his decision to abandon the attack.'

It was now almost dark, and Hudspeth surfaced the boat to set off back down the Altenfjord, with the CO standing on the coaming, keeping watch. Twice they had to dive when they spotted a patrol boat, but returned to the surface and carried on. At one point, to give Hudspeth a break from

navigating, they tried using the Direction Indicator, which was supposed to help them steer a straight course. Instead it turned the boat through 180 degrees, sending it heading back up the fjord again. Clearly that was another piece of equipment which wasn't working properly. Hudspeth therefore resumed his watch.

The headquarters of the 12th Submarine Flotilla was HMS *Varbel*, a former luxury spa hotel situated on a hill above Port Bannatyne on the Isle of Bute, in the Firth of Clyde. It was named after Commander Varley and Commander Bell, who helped bring the midget submarine force into being.

They reached the Smalfjord a little before dawn the next morning, Thursday, 23 September, but on finding it deserted, and visibility poor due to intermittent sleet and snow showers, Hudspeth decided to continue on the surface. They made good time through the narrow channel, and by mid-afternoon were in the Søroy Strait. By 6pm they reached the southern edge of the Søroy minefield, which they crossed without incident. By 11pm they were safely past all the obstacles, eager to make their rendezvous with *Thrasher*, their towing submarine. They ended up waiting throughout 24 September, until by evening Hudspeth decided the submarine wasn't going to show up.

The plan for Operation *Source* had specified that in this situation, the returning X-craft would head for a small bay on the north side of Søroy Island. They reached there at noon on 25 September, but found they were alone. Undeterred, they remained there until dawn on 27 September. As a final backup, the plan had called for a second rendezvous point at Ofjord, a little way down the coast of Søroy. If nobody was there, they decided to try to make it along the coast to the Soviet Union, or even across the Arctic Sea to Iceland. They reached the fjord that evening, and patrolled it for several hours. Eventually, Hudspeth declared he would give up the attempt in an hour – at 1am on 28 September.

An X-craft, photographed after being hauled out of the water onto the slip at HMS *Varbel*. This boat has been fitted with its side charges, which resembled low-slung panniers, one on each side of the midget submarine. The single bolt which held each charge in place also housed the charge's clockwork timer.

A moment or two before the deadline expired, they spotted movement in the water. It was the submarine *Stubborn*, surfacing so close to them that the X-craft was lifted by a wave and dropped onto the deck of the submarine. The four crewmen transferred to the larger submarine, and were greeted by Lieutenant Peter Philip and the passage crew of *X-7*, who would man the X-craft for the passage home. *Stubborn* headed back out to sea, setting a course for Shetland. Hudspeth and his three companions took the opportunity to sleep for 24 hours. On 3 October they relieved Philip's now weary passage crew, but shortly afterwards a storm arose, and the order was given to scuttle the X-craft. It was a sad business after going through so much, but there was no sensible alternative. That, effectively, was the end of the operation, rather than their landing in Lerwick, their transfer to another submarine or their homecoming reception at HMS *Varbel* on Bute.

The battleship

While it wasn't readily apparent at the time, *Tirpitz* had been very badly damaged. The hull was sound, apart from a metre-long hole on the port side of the forecastle, at the waterline. Her keel had been distorted slightly, and some of her bottom plates buckled. There had also been rapid flooding in the bottom compartments below the engine room, and above it in two of the battleship's three engine rooms. Further flooding took place aft, in the steering compartment. The real damage, though, was internal. The blast of the side charges had lifted the *Tirpitz* as much as 6ft out of the water, and the shock waves were felt throughout the ship for several seconds. Two of the three propeller shafts were buckled, and couldn't turn, and there was extensive shock damage to the engine and boiler mountings.

The result was that all three of its main engines had been put out of action due to the shock damage they suffered. Three of the four diesel generators were also damaged, and the turbine casings were cracked. A lot of the auxiliary machinery, such as the pumping system or boiler feeds, were also badly damaged. Effectively, *Tirpitz* was rendered immobile, and would remain so for several months. Even then she would only be able to move at a much-reduced speed. As the official British Admiralty report stated, based largely on evidence gathered by Norwegian Resistance, this damage would take at least six months to repair.

Above the waterline, most of the optics of her gunnery direction equipment had been shattered, and three of her four anti-aircraft directors were badly damaged. In addition, her port rudder had been jammed, one of her twin 15cm turrets on her port side (mounting PIII) was also locked solid, and the electronics in her anti-aircraft control centre were now beyond repair. This meant that at least for a while, *Tirpitz* was extremely vulnerable to enemy air attack. Almost all of her electrical system had been put out of action by the explosions, including her wireless and radar fittings. The lighting would be repaired quickly, but much of the other damage would take months to put right.

The *raison d'etre* of a battleship was her main armament. Without her big guns she was nothing but a floating target, with no real offensive power. Her four main twin 38cm gun turrets lay along the centreline, with two forward and two aft. These massive turrets sat on hundreds of large steel roller bearings. When the charges exploded, the blast lifted these 100-ton turrets upwards inside their turret housings. They then crashed down again on their roller mountings, causing extensive damage and jamming all four turrets. As a result, all four turrets were put out of action. 'Anton' and 'Caesar' turrets would remain inoperable for the rest of the battleship's life.

Fregattenkapitän (Commander) Eichler, the battleship's Engineering Officer, stated that repairs began in October 1943 and would continue until March 1944. The trouble was, without working engines, *Tirpitz* couldn't be moved down the Norwegian coast to a German shipyard. Even to attempt that would have been suicide, as it would merely invite coordinated mass attacks by the Home Fleet and RAF Bomber Command. So, she had to be repaired where she lay. That involved sending ships, workmen and equipment to the north of Norway, and doing what they could with the limited repair facilities available. As a result, the battleship was effectively put out of action for six months. This was the result that Winston Churchill had wanted. The 'Beast', as he called *Tirpitz*, had her teeth pulled, and would no longer present a major threat to the maritime lifeline of the Arctic Convoys.

ANALYSIS

The Admiralty would have to wait several days until they could learn how successful Operation *Source* had been. A PRU flight on 28 September revealed that the *Tirpitz* was riding low in the water and was surrounded by an oil slick, which was concentrated off her port side. Two days later came the news that *X-10* had been picked up by the submarine *Stubborn*, so her crew were available to give their reports. They told of the loud series of explosions at 8.12am on 22 September, and the likelihood that *Tirpitz* was badly damaged. Still, it was 8 October before Rear Admiral Barry wrote his report, based on an amalgam of photographic reconnaissance, Norwegian Resistance reports and the account provided by Lieutenant Hudspeth and his crew. He surmised that the damage caused may well be considerable. He was quite correct.

First of all, *Tirpitz* had been put out of action for the whole winter, so the Arctic Convoys could continue without fear of her making a sortie. A total of 16 convoys made the trip that winter, with relatively light losses. The loss of *Tirpitz* was a major blow to German naval power in the Arctic, and helped contribute to the lone sortie by the *Scharnhorst* that December. This led to her being cornered and sunk by warships of the Home Fleet on 26 December, in what became known as the Battle of North Cape.

Even after she was repaired, *Tirpitz* was not fully operational – the damage to her propeller shafts alone saw to that. Also, her propulsion system and main armament still required the attention of German shipyards, armament centres and steelworks. Therefore, her function as the core of a 'fleet in being' came to an end on 22 September. In order to resume that strategic role, *Tirpitz* would have to be moved south to the Baltic. This likelihood led to the heavy air attacks carried out by the Fleet Air Arm during the spring of 1944, which resulted in further damage. The final blow came at the hands of the Royal Air Force. During the autumn of 1944 a series of heavy bomber raids were carried out, using 'Tallboy' bombs weighing 12,000lb. These culminated in Operation *Catechism* on 12 November, when *Tirpitz* was finally sunk.

The one surviving intact X-craft, *X-24*, has been preserved, and is now on display in the Royal Navy Submarine Museum in Gosport. In this photograph, her port-side charge can be seen, bolted to the boat's hull. (Photograph by Eachan Hardie)

As for the X-craft, they would be replaced and further raids would be carried out, in Bergen and Singapore. By then, the lessons learned during Operation *Source* would make this new generation of X-craft both safer and more effective. During the attack on the German ships in the Altenfjord, the X-craft crews had been robbed of an even greater success by a number of problems. The first was the tow ropes used. All of the nylon ones worked perfectly – it was the man-made ones which proved faulty, leading directly to the loss of one X-craft and the near loss of two more. The passage could also have been shortened by using Shetland as a launching point for the operation, rather than the north-west of Scotland.

Then there were all the technical shortcomings of the boats themselves – the faulty gyro-compasses and periscopes, the leaking side ballast tanks, the erratic trim tanks and the various other equipment problems which limited the success of the operation. They would all be improved the next time an X-craft went into action, but that was small consolation for those who took part in Operation *Source*. However, given the problems they faced with faulty equipment, particularly their periscopes and gyro-compasses, it is even more astonishing that these X-craft crews achieved what they did. In the end, this was to a large extent down to training. These submariners had prepared for the operation for 18 months, and when the time came, their skill, as well as a huge amount of grit, perseverance and courage, helped achieve what many thought was impossible. They had put Germany's most powerful battleship out of action for what turned out to be the remainder of her career.

CONCLUSION

Afterwards, the Admiralty expressed its appreciation for the sacrifices made by the X-craft crews by giving them honours commensurate with their achievements. Donald Cameron and Godfrey Place were both awarded the Victoria Cross, Britain's highest military honour. Bob Aitken, Richard Kendall and John Lorimer received the Distinguished Service Order, while Ken Hudspeth was awarded the Distinguished Service Cross. Edmund Goddard was presented with the Conspicuous Gallantry Medal. All but Hudspeth received them after the war, following their release from German POW camps. It was unfortunate that Henry Henty-Creer and the crew of *X-5* received no posthumous awards, but then their contribution to the operation will forever be shrouded in mystery.

Perhaps the best summation of Operation *Source* came from the pen of Rear Admiral Barry in his dispatch, published in 1948: 'I cannot fully express my admiration for the three commanding officers, Lieuts. H. Henty-Creer RNVR, D. Cameron RNVR and B.G. Place RN, and the crews of *X-5*, *6* and *7*, who pressed home their attack and who failed to return. In the full knowledge of the hazards that they were to encounter, these gallant crews penetrated into a heavily defended fleet anchorage. There, with cool courage and determination, and in spite of all the modern devices that ingenuity devised for their detection and destruction, they pressed home their attack to the full.' He continued: 'It is clear that courage and enterprise of the very highest order was shown by these gallant gentlemen, whose daring attack will surely go down in history as one of the most courageous acts of all time.'

FURTHER READING

Bishop, Patrick, *Target Tirpitz*, Harper Press, London (2012)

Gallagher, Thomas, *Against All Odds: Midget Submarines against the Tirpitz*, Macdonald & Co. Ltd, London (1971)

Gardiner, Robert (ed.), *Conway's All the World's Fighting Ships*, Conway Maritime Press, London (1980)

Gröner, Erich, *German Warships, 1815–1945*, Vol. 1, *Major Surface Vessels*, Conway Maritime Press, London (1983)

Grove, Eric, *Sea Battles in Close-Up, World War* 2, Vol. 2, Ian Allen Ltd, Shepperton (1993)

Howard, Peter, *Underwater Raid on Tirpitz*, Ian Allen Publishing Special Operations Series, Hersham (2006)

Jacobsen, Alf R., *X-Craft Versus Tirpitz: The Mystery of the Missing* X5, Sutton Publishing, Stroud (2006)

Kemp, Paul, *Midget Submarines of the Second World War*, Chatham Publishing, London (1999)

Kemp, Paul, *Underwater Warriors*, Arms & Armour Press, London (1996)

Kennedy, Ludovic, *Menace: The Life and Death of the Tirpitz*, Sidgwick & Jackson Ltd, London (1979)

Watkins, Paul, *Midget Submarine Commander: The Life of Godfrey Place VC*, Pen & Sword, Barnsley (2012)

Watson, C. E. T. & Benson, James, *Above us the Waves: The Story of Midget Submarines and Human Torpedoes*, Harrap & Co. Ltd, London (1953)

Whitley, M. J., *Battleships of World War Two*, Arms & Armour Press, London (1998)

Zetterling, Niklas & Tamelander, Michael, *Tirpitz: The Life and Death of Germany's Last Super Battleship*, Casemate Publishing, Newbury (2009)

INDEX

References to images are in **bold**.